Hebraic Grammar

Fabre D'Olivet

Kessinger Publishing's Rare Reprints

Thousands of Scarce and Hard-to-Find Books on These and other Subjects!

- Americana
- Ancient Mysteries
- Animals
- Anthropology
- Architecture
- Arts
- Astrology
- Bibliographies
- Biographies & Memoirs
- Body, Mind & Spirit
- Business & Investing
- Children & Young Adult
- Collectibles
- Comparative Religions
- Crafts & Hobbies
- Earth Sciences
- Education
- Ephemera
- Fiction
- Folklore
- Geography
- Health & Diet
- History
- Hobbies & Leisure
- Humor
- Illustrated Books
- Language & Culture
- Law
- Life Sciences
- Literature
- Medicine & Pharmacy
- Metaphysical
- Music
- Mystery & Crime
- Mythology
- Natural History
- Outdoor & Nature
- Philosophy
- Poetry
- Political Science
- Science
- Psychiatry & Psychology
- Reference
- Religion & Spiritualism
- Rhetoric
- Sacred Books
- Science Fiction
- Science & Technology
- Self-Help
- Social Sciences
- Symbolism
- Theatre & Drama
- Theology
- Travel & Explorations
- War & Military
- Women
- Yoga
- *Plus Much More!*

We kindly invite you to view our catalog list at:
http://www.kessinger.net

THIS ARTICLE WAS EXTRACTED FROM THE BOOK:

Hebraic Tongue Restored Part 1

BY THIS AUTHOR:

Fabre D'Olivet

ISBN 0766126064

READ MORE ABOUT THE BOOK AT OUR WEB SITE:

http://www.kessinger.net

OR ORDER THE COMPLETE
BOOK FROM YOUR FAVORITE STORE

ISBN 0766126064

Because this article has been extracted from a parent book, it may have non-pertinent text at the beginning or end of it.

Any blank pages following the article are necessary for our book production requirements. The article herein is complete.

Hebraic Grammar

HEBRAIC GRAMMAR

CHAPTER I.

GENERAL PRINCIPLES.

§ I.

THE REAL PURPOSE OF THIS GRAMMAR.

Long ago it was said, that grammar was the art of writing and of speaking a tongue correctly: but long ago it ought also to have been considered that this definition good for living tongues was of no value applied to dead ones.

In fact, what need is there of knowing how to speak and even write (if composing is what is meant by writing) Sanskrit, Zend, Hebrew and other tongues of this nature? Does one not feel that it is not a question of giving to modern thoughts an exterior which has not been made for them; but, on the contrary, of discovering under a worn-out exterior ancient thoughts worthy to be revived under more modern forms? Thoughts are for all time, all places and all men. It is not thus with the tongues which express them. These tongues are appropriate to the customs, laws, understanding and periods of the ages; they become modified in proportion as they advance in the centuries; they follow the course of the civilization of peoples. When one of these has ceased to be spoken it can only be understood through the writings which have survived. To continue to speak or even to write it when its genius is extinguished, is to wish to resuscitate a dead body; to affect the Roman toga, or to appear in the streets of Paris in the robe of an ancient Druid.

I must frankly say, despite certain scholastic precedents being offended by my avowal, that I cannot approve of those sorry compositions, whether in prose or in verse, where modern Europeans rack their brains to clothe the forms long since gone, with English, German or French thoughts. I do not doubt that this tendency everywhere in public instruction is singularly harmful to the advancement of studies, and that the constraint of modern ideas to adapt themselves to ancient forms is an attitude which checks what the ancient ideas might pass on in the modern forms. If Hesiod and Homer are not perfectly understood; if Plato himself offers obscurity, for what reason is this so? For no other reason save that instead of seeking to understand their tongue, one has foolishly attempted to speak or write it.

The grammar of the ancient tongues is not therefore, either the art of speaking or even of writing them, since the sound is extinct and since the signs have lost their relations with the ideas; but the grammar of these tongues is the art of understanding them, of penetrating the genius which has presided at their formation, of going back to their source, and by the aid of the ideas which they have preserved and the knowledge which they have procured, of enriching modern idioms and enlightening their progress.

So then, while proposing to give an Hebraic grammar, my object is assuredly not to teach anyone either to speak or to write this tongue; that preposterous care should be left to the rabbis of the synagogues. These rabbis, after tormenting themselves over the value of the accents and the vowel points, have been able to continue their cantillation of certain barbarous sounds; they have been indeed able to compose some crude books, as heterogeneous in substance as in form, but the fruit of so many pains has been to ignore utterly the signification of the sole Book which remained to them, and to make themselves more and more incapable of defending their lawmaker, one of the noblest men that the earth has produced, from the increased attacks that have never ceased to be directed against him by those who knew him only through the thick clouds with which he had been enveloped by his translators.* For, as I have sufficiently intimated, the Book of Moses has never been accurately translated. The most ancient versions of the Sepher which we possess, such as those of the Samaritans, the Chaldaic Targums, the Greek version of the Septuagint and the Latin Vulgate, render only the grossest and most exterior forms without attaining to the spirit which animates them in the original. I might compare them appropriately with those disguises which were used in the ancient mysteries,[1] or even with those symbolic figures which were used by the initiates; the small figures of satyrs and of Sileni that were brought from Eleusis. There was nothing more absurd and grotesque than their outward appearance, upon opening them, however, by means of a secret spring, there were found all the divinities of Olympus. Plato speaks of this pleasing allegory in his dialogue of the Banquet and applies it to Socrates through the medium of Alcibiades.

It is because they saw only these exterior and material forms of the Sepher, and because they knew not how to make use of the secret which could disclose its spiritual and divine forms, that the Sadducees fell into materialism and denied the immortality of the soul.[2] It is well known how much Moses has been calumniated by modern philosophers upon the same subject.[3] Fréret has not failed to quote all those who, like him, have ranked him among the materialists.

* The most famous heresiarchs, Valentine, Marcion and Manes rejected scornfully the writings of Moses which they believed emanated from an evil principle.

[1] Apul. I. XL.
[2] Joseph. *Antiq*. I. XIII. g.
[3] Fréret: *des Apol. de la Rel. chrét*. ch. II.

When I say that the rabbis of the synagogues have put themselves beyond the state of defending their lawgiver, I wish it to be understood that I speak only of those who, holding to the most meticulous observances of the *Masorah*, have never penetrated the secret of the sanctuary. Doubtless there are many to whom the genius of the Hebraic tongue is not foreign. But a sacred duty imposes upon them an inviolable silence.[4] It is said, that they hold the version of the Hellenists in abomination. They attribute to it all the evils which they have suffered. Alarmed at its use against them by the Christians in the early ages of the Church, their superiors forbade them thereafter to write the Sepher in other characters than the Hebraic, and doomed to execration those among them who should betray the mysteries and teach the Christians the principles of their tongue. One ought therefore to mistrust their exterior doctrine. Those of the rabbis who were initiated kept silence, as Moses, son of Maimon, called Maimonides, expressly said:[5] those who were not, had as little real knowledge of Hebrew, as the least learned of the Christians. They wavered in the same incertitude over the meaning of the words, and this incertitude was such that they were ignorant even of the name of some of the animals of which it was forbidden them, or commanded by the Law, to eat.[6] Richard Simon who has furnished me with this remark, never wearies of repeating how obscure is the Hebraic tongue:[7] he quotes Saint Jerome and Luther, who are agreed in saying, that the words of this tongue are equivocal to such an extent that it is often impossible to determine the meaning.[8] Origen, according to him, was persuaded of this truth; Calvin felt it and Cardinal Cajetan himself, was convinced.[9] It

[4] Richard Simon, *Hist. Crit.* L. I. ch. 17
[5] *Mor. Nebuc.* P. II. ch. 29.
[6] Bochart: *de Sacr. animal.*
[7] *Ibid.* I. III. ch. 2.
[8] Hieron. *Apelog. adv. Ruff.* I. 1. Luther, *Comment. Genes.*
[9] Cajetan, *Comment. in Psalm.*

PURPOSE OF THIS GRAMMAR

was Father Morin who took advantage of this obscurity to consider the authors of the Septuagint version as so many prophets;[10] for, he said, God had no other means of fixing the signification of the Hebrew words.

This reason of Father Morin, somewhat far from being decisive, has not hindered the real thinkers, and Richard Simon particularly, from earnestly wishing that the Hebraic tongue lost for so long à time, might finally be reëstablished.[11] He did not conceal the immense difficulties that such an undertaking entailed. He saw clearly that it would be necessary to study this tongue in a manner very different from the one hitherto adopted, and far from making use of the grammars and dictionaries available, he regarded them, on the contrary, as the most dangerous obstacles; for, he says, these grammars and these dictionaries are worth nothing. All those who have had occasion to apply their rules and to make use of their interpretations have felt their insufficiency.[12] Forster who had seen the evil sought in vain the means to remedy it. He lacked the force for that: both time and men, as well as his own prejudices were too much opposed.*

I have said enough in my Dissertation concerning what had been the occasion and the object of my studies. When I conceived the plan with which I am now occupied, I knew neither Richard Simon nor Forster, nor any of the thinkers who, agreeing in regarding the Hebraic tongue as lost, had made endeavours for, or had hoped to succeed in its reëstablishment; but truth is absolute, and it is truth which has engaged me in a difficult undertaking; it is truth which will sustain me in it; I now pursue my course.

[10] *Exercit. Bibl.* L. I. ex. VI. ch. 2.
[11] *Hist. crit.* I. III. ch. 2.
[12] *Hist. Crit.* I. III. ch. 3.

* The rabbis themselves have not been more fortunate, as one can see in the grammar of Abraham de Balmes and in several other works.

§ II.

ETYMOLOGY AND DEFINITION.

The word *grammar* has come down to us from the Greeks, through the Latins; but its origin goes back much further. Its real etymology is found in the root קר, כר, גר (*gre, cre, kre*), which in Hebrew, Arabic or Chaldaic, presents always the idea of engraving, of character or of writing, and which as verb is used to express, according to the circumstances, the action of engraving, of characterizing, of writing, of proclaiming, of reading, of declaiming, etc. The Greek word γραμματική signifies properly the science of characters, that is to say, of the characteristic signs by means of which man expresses his thought.

As has been very plainly seen by Court de Gébelin, he who, of all the archæologists has penetrated deepest into the genius of tongues, there exist two kinds of grammars: the one, universal, and the other, particular. The universal grammar reveals the spirit of man in general; the particular grammars develop the individual spirit of a people, indicate the state of its civilization, its knowledge and its prejudices. The first, is founded upon nature, and rests upon the basis of the universality of things; the others, are modified according to opinion, places and times. All the particular grammars have a common basis by which they resemble each other and which constitutes the universal grammar from which they emanate:[13] for, says this laborious writer, "these particular grammars, after having received the life of the universal grammar, react in their turn upon their

[13] *Mond. prim. Gramm. univ.* t. I, ch. 13, 14 et 15.

ETYMOLOGY AND DEFINITION

mother, to which they give new force to bring forth stronger and more fruitful off-shoots."

I quote here the opinion of this man whose grammatical knowledge cannot be contested, in order to make it understood, that wishing to initiate my readers into the inner genius of the Hebraic tongue, I must needs give to that tongue its own grammar; that is to say, its idiomatic and primitive grammar, which, holding to the universal grammar by the points most radical and nearest to its basis, will nevertheless, be very different from the particular grammars upon which it has been modelled up to this time.

This grammar will bear no resemblance to that of the Greeks or that of the Latins, because it is neither the idiom of Plato nor that of Titus Livius which I wish to teach, but that of Moses. I am convinced that the principal difficulties in studying Hebrew are due to the adoption of Latin forms, which have caused a simple and easy tongue to become a species of scholastic phantom whose difficulty is proverbial.

For, I must say with sincerity, that Hebrew is not such as it has ordinarily been represented. It is necessary to set aside the ridiculous prejudice that has been formed concerning it and be fully persuaded that the first difficulties of the characters being overcome, all that is necessary is six months closely sustained application.

I have said enough regarding the advantages of this study, so that I need not dwell further on this subject. I shall only repeat, that without the knowledge of this typical tongue, one of the fundamental parts of universal grammar will always be unknown, and it will be impossible to proceed with certainty in the vast and useful field of etymology.

As my intention is therefore to differ considerably from the method of the Hebraists I shall avoid entering into the detail of their works. Besides they are sufficiently well known. I shall limit myself here to indicate summarily, those of the rabbis whose ideas offer some analogy to mine.

The Hebraic tongue having become absolutely lost during the captivity of Babylon, all grammatical system was also lost. From that time nothing is found by which we can infer that the Jews possessed a grammar. At least, it is certain that the crude dialect which was current in Jerusalem at the time of Jesus Christ, and which is found employed in the Talmud of that city, reads more like a barbarous jargon than like an idiom subject to fixed rules. If anything leads me to believe that this degenerated tongue preserved a sort of grammatical system, before the captivity and while Hebrew was still the vulgar tongue, it is the fact that a great difference is found in the style of writing of certain writers. Jeremiah, for example, who was a man of the people, wrote evidently without any understanding of his tongue, not concerning himself either with gender, number or verbal tense; whilst Isaiah, on the contrary, whose instruction had been most complete, observes rigorously these modifications and prides himself on writing with as much elegance as purity.

But at last, as I have just said, all grammatical system was lost with the Hebraic tongue. The most learned Hebraists are agreed in saying, that although, from the times of the earliest Hellenist interpreters, it had been the custom to explain the Hebrew, there had been, however, no grammar reduced to an art.

The Jews, dispersed and persecuted after the ruin of Jerusalem, were buried in ignorance for a long time. The school of Tiberias, where Saint Jerome had gone, possessed no principle of grammar. The Arabs were the first to remedy this defect. Europe was at that time plunged in darkness. Arabia, placed between Asia and Africa, reanimated for a moment their ancient splendour.

The rabbis are all of this sentiment. They assert that those of their nation who began to turn their attention to grammar did so only in imitation of the Arabs. The first books which they wrote on grammar were in Arabic. After Saadia-Gaon, who appears to have laid the foundation, the most ancient is Juda-Hayyuj. The opinion of the latter is remarkable.[14] He is the first to speak, in his work, of the letters which are hidden and those which are added. The greatest secret of the Hebraic tongue consists, according to him, of knowing how to distinguish these sorts of letters, and to mark precisely those which are of the substance of the words, and those which are not. He states that the secret of these letters is known to but few persons, and in this he takes up again the ignorance of the rabbis of his time, who, lacking this understanding were unable to reduce the words to their true roots to discover their meaning.

The opinion of Juda-Hayyuj is confirmed by that of Jonah, one of the best grammarians the Jews have ever had. He declares at the beginning of his book, that the Hebraic tongue has been lost, and that it has been reëstablished as well as possible by means of the neighbouring idioms. He reprimands the rabbis sharply for putting among the number of radicals, many letters which are only accessories. He lays great stress upon the intrinsic value of each character, relates carefully their various peculiarities and shows their different relations with regard to the verb.

The works of Juda-Hayyuj and those of Jonah have never been printed, although they have been translated from the Arabic into rabbinical Hebrew. The learned Pocock who has read the books of Jonah in Arabic, under the name of Ebn-Jannehius, quotes them with praise. Aben Ezra has followed the method indicated by these two ancient grammarians in his two books entitled *Zahot* and *Moznayim*. David Kimchi diviates more. The Christian Hebraists have followed Kimchi more willingly than they have Aben Ezra, as much on account of the clear-

[14] Richard Simon. *Hist. Crit.* L. I. ch. 31.

ness of his style, as of his method which is easier. But in this they have committed a fault which they have aggravated further by adopting, without examining them, nearly all of the opinions of Elijah Levita, ambitious and systematic writer, and regarded as a deserter and apostate by his nation.

I dispense with mentioning other Jewish grammarians.* I have only entered into certain details with regard to Juda-Hayyuj, Jonah and Aben Ezra, because I have strong reasons for thinking, as will be shown in the development of the work, that they have penetrated to a certain point, the secret of the Essenian sanctuary, either by the sole force of their genius or by the effect of some oral communication.

* Although Maimonides is not, properly speaking, a grammarian, his way of looking at things coincides too well with my principles to pass over them entirely in silence. This judicious writer teaches that as the greater part of the words offer, in Hebrew, a generic, universal and almost always uncertain meaning, it is necessary to understand the sphere of activity which they embrace in their diverse acceptations, so as to apply that which agrees best with the matter of which he is treating. After having pointed out, that in this ancient idiom, very few words exist for an endless series of things, he recommends making a long study of it, and having the attention always fixed upon the particular subject to which the word is especially applied. He is indefatigable in recommending, as can be seen in the fifth chapter of his book, long meditation before restricting the meaning of a word, and above all, renunciation of all prejudices if one would avoid falling into error.

§ III.

DIVISION OF GRAMMAR:

PARTS OF SPEECH.

I have announced that I was about to reëstablish the Hebraic tongue in its own grammar. I claim a little attention, since the subject is new, and I am obliged to present certain ideas but little familiar, and also since it is possible that there might not be time for me to develop them to the necessary extent.

The modern grammarians have varied greatly concerning the number of what they call, parts of speech. Now, they understand by parts of speech, the classified materials of speech; for if the idea is one, they say, the expression is divisible, and from this divisibility arises necessarily in the signs, diverse modifications and words of many kinds.

These diverse modifications and these words of many kinds have, as I have said, tried the sagacity of the grammarian. Plato and his disciples only recognized two kinds, the noun and the verb;[15] neglecting in this, the more ancient opinion which, according to the testimony of Dionysius of Halicarnassus and Quintilian, admitted three, the noun, the verb and the conjunction.[16] Aristotle, more to draw away from the doctrine of Plato than to approach that of the ancients, counted four: the noun, the verb, the article and the conjunction.[17] The Stoics acknowledged five, distinguishing the noun as proper and appellative.[18] Soon the Greek grammarians, and after

[15] Plat. *in Sophist*. Prisc. L. II. Apollon. *Syn.*
[16] Denys Halyc, *de Struct. orat.* 2. Quint. *Inst.* L. I. ch. 4.
[17] Arist. *Poet.* ch. 20.
[18] Diog. Laert. L. VIII, §. 57.

them the Latins, separated the pronoun from the noun, the adverb from the verb, the preposition from the conjunction and the interjection from the article. Among the moderns, some have wished to distinguish the adjective from the noun; others, to join them; again, some have united the article with the adjective, and others, the pronoun with the noun. Nearly all have brought into their work the spirit of the system or prejudices of their school. Court de Gébelin [19] who should have preferred the simplicity of Plato to the profusion of the Latin grammatists, has had the weakness to follow the latter and even to surpass them, by counting ten parts of speech and giving the participle as one of them.

As for me, without further notice of these vain disputes, I shall recognize in the Hebraic tongue only three parts of speech produced by a fourth which they in their turn produce. These three parts are the Noun, the Verb, and the Relation: שם *shem*, פעל *phahal*, מלה *millah*. The fourth is the Sign, אות *aoth*.*

Before examining these three parts of speech, the denomination of which is quite well known, let us see what

[19] *Gramm. univ.* L. II. ch. 2. 3 et 4.

* An English grammarian named Harris, better rhetorician than able dialectician, has perhaps believed himself nearer to Plato and Aristotle, by recognizing at first only two things in nature, the *substance* and the *attribute*, and by dividing the words into *principals* and *accessories*. According to him one should regard as principal words, the *substantive* and the *attributive*, in other words, the noun and the verb; as accessory words, the *definitive* and the *connective*, that is to say, the article and the conjunction. Thus this writer, worthy pupil of Locke, but far from being a disciple of Plato, regards the verb only as an attribute of the noun. "*To think*," he said, "is an attribute of man; *to be white*, is an attribute of the swan; *to fly*, an attribute of the eagle, etc." (*Hermes*, L. I. ch. 3.) It is difficult by making such grammars, to go far in the understanding of speech. To deny the absolute existence of the verb, or to make it an attribute of the substance, is to be very far from Plato, who comprises in it the very essence of language; but very near to Cabanis who makes the soul a faculty of the body.

is the fourth, which I have just mentioned for the first time.

By *Sign,* I understand all the exterior means of which man makes use to manifest his ideas. The elements of the sign are voice, gesture and traced characters: its materials, sound, movement and light. The universal grammar ought especially to be occupied with, and to understand its elements: it ought, according to Court de Gébelin, to distinguish the sounds of the voice, to regulate the gestures, and preside at the invention of the characters.[20] The more closely a particular grammar is related to the universal grammar, the more it has need to be concerned with the *sign.* This is why we shall give very considerable attention to this in regard to one of its elements,— the traced characters; for, as far as the voice and gesture are concerned, they have disappeared long ago and the traces they have left are too vague to be taken up by the Hebraic grammar, such as I have conceived it to be.

Every sign produced exteriorly is a noun; for otherwise it would be nothing. It is, therefore, the noun which is the basis of language; it is, therefore, the noun which furnishes the substance of the verb, that of the relation, and even that of the sign which has produced it. The noun is everything for exterior man, everything that he can understand by means of his senses. The verb is conceived only by the mind, and the relation is only an abstraction of thought.

There exists only one sole Verb, absolute, independent, creative and inconceivable for man himself whom it penetrates, and by whom it allows itself to be felt: it is the verb *to be-being,* expressed in Hebrew by the intellectual sign ו *o,* placed between a double root of life הוה, *hoeh.*

It is this verb, unique and universal, which, penetrating a mass of innumerable nouns that receive their

---

[20] *Gramm. univ.* L. I, ch. 8. et 9.

existence from the sign, forms particular verbs. It is the universal soul. The particular verbs are only animated nouns.

The relations are abstracted by thought from signs, nouns or verbs, and incline toward the sign as toward their common origin.

We shall examine in particular each of these four parts of speech in the following order: the *Sign*, the *Relation*, the *Noun* and the *Verb*, concerning which I have as yet given only general ideas. In terminating this chapter, the Hebrew alphabet, which it is indispensable to understand before going further, is now added. I have taken pains to accompany it with another comparative alphabet of Samaritan, Syriac, Arabic and Greek characters; so as to facilitate the reading of words in these tongues, which I shall be compelled to cite in somewhat large number, in my radical vocabulary and in my notes upon the Cosmogony of Moses.

It must be observed, as regards the comparative Alphabet, that it follows the order of the Hebraic characters. This order is the same for the Samaritan and Syriac; but as the Arabs and Greeks have greatly inverted this order, I have been obliged to change somewhat the idiomatic arrangement of their characters, to put them in relation to those of the Hebrews. When I have encountered in these last two tongues, characters which have no analogues in the first three, I have decided to place them immediately after those with which they offer the closest relations.

Hebraic Alphabet
and
Comparative Alphabet

HEBRAIC ALPHABET

א	A, a.	as mother-vowel, this is *a*: as consonant, it is a very soft aspiration.
ב	B, b, bh.	English *b*.
ג	G, g, gh.	English *g* before a, o, u.
ד	D, d, dh.	English *d*.
ה	H, hè, h.	as mother-vowel, this is *è*: as consonant, it is a simple aspiration: *h*.
ו ן ף	O, o, W or U, u, y.	as mother-vowel, this is *o, u, ou*: as consonant, it is *v, w* or *f*.
ז	Z, z.	English *z*.
ח	H, hê, h, ch.	as mother-vowel, this is *hê*: as consonant, it is a chest aspiration: *h*, or *ch*.
ט	T, t.	English *t*.
י	I, i, J, j.	as mother-vowel, this is *i* or *aï*: as consonant, it is a whispering aspiration: *j*.
כ ך	C, c, ch.	German *ch*, Spanish iota, Greek χ.
ל	L, l.	} same as English analogues.
מ ם	M, m.	
נ ן	N, n.	
ס	S, s.	
ע	H, ho, gh, gho	as mother-vowel, it is the Arabic ع *ho*: as consonant, it is a guttural aspiration, the nasal *gh*, the Arabic غ.
פ	PH, ph.	Greek φ.
צ ץ	TZ, tz.	} Same as English.
ק	K, k, qu.	
ר	R, r.	
ש	SH, sh.	French *ch* or English *sh*.
ת	TH, th.	English *th* or Greek θ.

Comparative Alphabet

Hebrew	Samaritan	Syriac	Arabic	Greek	French
א aleph.	ࠀ	ܐ	ا	A α	A a.
ב beth.	ࠁ	ܒ	ب	B β ϐ	B b.
ג ghimel.	ࠂ	ܓ	ج	Γ γ	G g gh.
ד daleth.	ࠃ	ܕ	د	Δ δ	D d.
			ذ		DZ dz, d weak.
			ض ظ		DH dh, d strong.
ה hè.	ࠄ	ܗ	ه	E ε	E, Hè.
ו wao.	ࠅ	ܘ	و	O o, Ω ω, Υ υ	O o, OU ou, U u.
ז zaïn.	ࠆ	ܙ	ز	Z ζ	Z z.
ח heth.	ࠇ	ܚ	ح	H η	Ḣ hė.
			خ	X χ	CH ch.
ט teth.	ࠈ	ܛ	ت	T τ	T t.
			ط		TH th, t strong.
י ïod.	ࠉ	ܝ	ي	I ι	I i.
כ ך caph.	ࠊ	ܟ	ق		KH kh.
ל lamed.	ࠋ	ܠ	ل	Λ λ	L l.
מ ם mëm.	ࠌ	ܡ	م	M μ	M. m.
נ ן noun.	ࠍ	ܢ	ن	N ν	N n.
ס samech.	ࠎ	ܣ	س	Σ ς σ	S s.
			ص		SS ss, s strong.
ע haïn.	ࠏ	ܥ	ع	ΟΥ υ	Ḣ ho, wh.
			غ		GH gh.
פ ף phè.	ࠐ	ܦ	ف	Φ φ	PH ph, F f.
				Π π ϖ	P p.
				Ψ ψ	PS ps.
צ ץ tzad.	ࠑ	ܨ	ط		TZ tz.
ק coph.	ࠒ	ܩ	ك	K κ	C c, K k, Q q.
ר resch.	ࠓ	ܪ	ر	P ρ	R r.
ש shin.	ࠔ	ܫ	ش		SH sh.
ת thao.	ࠕ	ܬ	ث	Θ θ	TH th.

CHAPTER II.

SIGNS CONSIDERED AS CHARACTERS.

§ I.

HEBRAIC ALPHABET: ITS VOWELS: ITS ORIGIN.

Before examining what the signification of the characters which we have just laid down can be, it is well to see what is their relative value.

The first division which is established here is that which distinguishes them as vowels and as consonants. I would have much to do if I related in detail all that has been said, for and against the existence of the Hebraic vowels. These insipid questions might have been solved long ago, if those who had raised them had taken the trouble to examine seriously the object of their dispute. But that was the thing concerning which they thought the least. Some had only a scholastic erudition which took cognizance of the material of the tongue; others, who had a critical faculty and a philosophic mind were often ignorant even of the form of the Oriental characters.

I ask in all good faith, how the alphabet of the Hebrews could have lacked the proper characters to designate the vowels, since it is known that the Egyptians who were their masters in all the sciences, possessed these characters and made use of them, according to the report of Demetrius of Phalereus, to note their music and to solmizate it; since it is known, by the account of Horus-Apollonius, that there were seven of these characters;[1] since it is known that the Phœnicians, close neighbours of the Hebrews, used these vocal characters to designate the seven planets.[2] Porphyry testifies positively to this in his

[1] *Hyeroglyph.* L. II. 29.
[2] Cedren. p. 169.

Commentary upon the grammarian Dionysius Thrax,[3] which confirms unquestionably, the inscription found at Milet, and concerning which we possess a learned dissertation by Barthelemy.[4] This inscription includes invocations addressed to the seven planetary spirits. Each spirit is designated by a name composed of seven vowels and beginning with the vowel especially consecrated to the planet which it governs.

Let us hesitate no longer to say that the Hebrew alphabet has characters whose primitive purpose was to distinguish the vowels; these characters are seven in number.

א soft vowel, represented by *a*.

ה stronger vowel, represented by *e, h*.

ח very strong pectoral vowel, represented by *e, h, ch*.

ו indistinct, dark vowel, represented by *ou, u, y*.

ׂו brilliant vowel, represented by *o*.

י hard vowel, represented by *i*.

ע deep and guttural vowel, represented by *ho, who*.

Besides these vocal characters, it is further necessary to know that the Hebrew alphabet admits a vowel which I shall call consonantal or vague, because it is inherent in the consonant, goes with it, is not distinguishable, and attaches to it a sound always implied. This sound is indifferently *a, e, o*, for we ought not to believe that the vocal sound which accompanies the consonants has been as fixed in the ancient tongues of the Orient as it has become in the modern tongues of Europe. The word מלך, which signifies a *king*, is pronounced indifferently *malach, melech, moloch*, and even *milich;* with a faint sound of the voice. This indifference in the vocal sound would not have existed if a written vowel had been inserted between the consonants which compose it; then the sound would have become fixed and striking, but of

---

[3] *Mém. de Gotting.* T. I. p. 251. *sur l'ouvrage de Démétrius de Phal* Περὶ Ἑρμηνείας.

[4] *Mém. de l'Acad. des Belles-Lettres*, T. XLI. p. 514.

ten the sense would also have been changed. Thus, for example, the word מלך, receiving the mother vowel א, as in מלאך, signifies no longer simply *a king*, but a divine, eternal emanation; *an eon, an angel.*

When it was said that the Hebrew words were written without vowels, it was not understood, and Boulanger who has committed this mistake in his encyclopædic article, proves to me by this alone, that he was ignorant of the tongue of which he wrote.

All Hebrew words have vowels expressed or implied, that is to say, mother vowels or consonantal vowels. In the origin of this tongue, or rather in the origin of the Egyptian tongue from which it is derived, the sages who created the alphabet which it has inherited, attached a vocal sound to each consonant, a sound nearly always faint, without aspiration, and passing from the *æ* to the *œ*, or from the *a* to the *e*, without the least difficulty; they reserved the written characters for expressing the sounds more fixed, aspirate or striking. This literal alphabet, whose antiquity is unknown, has no doubt come down to us as far as its material characters are concerned; but as to its spirit, it has come down in sundry imitations that have been transmitted to us by the Samaritans, Chaldeans, Syrians and even the Arabs.

The Hebraic alphabet is that of the Chaldeans. The characters are remarkable for their elegance of form and their clearness. The Samaritan much more diffuse, much less easy to read, is obviously anterior and belongs to a more rude people. The savants who have doubted the anteriority of the Samaritan character had not examined it with sufficient attention. They have feared besides, that if once they granted the priority of the character, they would be forced to grant the priority of the text; but this is a foolish fear. The Samaritan text, although its alphabet may be anterior to the Chaldaic alphabet, is nevertheless only a simple copy of the Sepher of Moses, which the politics of the kings of Assyria caused to pass into Samaria, as I have already said in my Dissertation; if this copy differs it is because the priest who was charged with it, as one reads in the Book of Kings,[5] either conformed to the ideas of the Samaritans with whom he wished to keep up the schism, or he consulted manuscripts by no means accurate. It would be ridiculous to say with Leclerc,[6] that this priest was the author of the entire Sepher; but there is not the least absurdity in thinking that he was the author of the principal different readings which are encountered there; for the interest of the court of Assyria which sent him was, that he should estrange as much as possible the Samaritans and the Jews, and that he should stir up their mutual animosity by all manner of means.

It is therefore absolutely impossible to deny the Chaldean origin of the characters of which the Hebraic alphabet is composed today. The very name of this alphabet demonstrates it sufficiently. This name written thus כתיבה אשורית (*chathibah ashourith*) signifies, Assyrian writing: an epithet known to all the rabbis, and to which following the genius of the Hebraic tongue, nothing prevents adding the formative and local sign מ to obtain כתיבה מאשורית (*chathibah mashourith*), writing in the Assyrian style. This is the quite simple denomination of this alphabet; a denomination in which, through a very singular abuse of words, this same Elijah Levita, of whom I have had occasion to speak, insisted on seeing the Masorites of Tiberias; thus confusing beyond any criticism, the ancient Mashorah with the modern Masorah, and the origin of the vowel points with rules infinitely newer, that are followed in the synagogues relative to their employment.*

[5] *Kings* L. II. ch. 17. v. 27.

[6] Leclerc: *Sentimens de quelq. theol. de Hollande.* L. VI.

* No one is ignorant of the famous disputes which were raised among the savants of the last centuries concerning the origin of the vowel points. These points had always been considered as contem-

§ II.

ORIGIN OF THE VOWEL POINTS.

Thus therefore, the Hebraic alphabet, whatever might have been the form of its characters at the very remote epoch when Moses wrote his work, had seven written vowels: א, ה, ח, ו, ו, י, ע; besides a vague vowel attached to each consonant which I have called on account of this, consonantal vowel. But by a series of events which hold to principles too far from my subject to be explained here, the sound of the written vowels became altered, materialized, hardened as it were, and changed in such a way that the characters which expressed them were conporaries of the Hebraic characters and belonging to the same inventors; when suddenly, about the middle of the sixteenth century, Elijah Levita attacked their antiquity and attributed the invention to the rabbis of the school of Tiberias who flourished about the fifth century of our era. The entire synagogue rose in rebellion against him, and regarded him as a blasphemer. His system would have remained buried in obscurity, if Louis Cappell, pastor of the Protestant Church at Saumur, after having passed thirty-six years of his life noting down the different readings of the Hebraic text, disheartened at being unable to understand it, had not changed his idea concerning these same points which had caused him so much trouble and had not taken to heart the opinion of Elijah Levita.

Buxtorf, who had just made a grammar, opposed both Elijah Levita and Cappell, and started a war in which all the Hebrew scholars have taken part during the last two centuries, never asking themselves, in their disputes for or against the points, what was the real point of question. Now, this is the real point. Elijah Levita did not understand Hebrew, or if he did understand it, he was very glad to profit by an equivocal word of that tongue to start the war which drew attention to him.

The word אשורי (*ashouri*), signifies in Hebrew, as in Chaldaic, *Assyrian*, that which belongs to Assyria, its root שר or שור indicates all that which tends to rule, to be lifted up; all that which emanates from an original principle of force, of grandeur and of *éclat*. The fused with the other consonants. The vowels א, ה and ח offered only an aspiration more or less strong, being deprived of all vocal sound; ו and ו became the consonants *v* and *w*; י was pronounced *ji*, and ע took a raucous and nasal accent.*

If, as has very well been said by the ancients, the vowels are the soul and the consonants the body of the words,[7] the Hebraic writing and all which, generally

alphabet of which Esdras made use in transcribing the Sepher, was called כתיבה אשורית *Assyrian writing*, or in a figurative sense, sovereign, primordial, original writing. The addition of the sign מ having reference to the intensive verbal form, only gives more force to the expression. כתיבה מאשורית, signifies therefore, *writing in the manner of the Assyrian*, or writing emanated from the sovereign radiant principle. This is the origin of the first *mashorah*, the real mashorah to which both the Hebraic characters and vowel points which accompany them must be related.

But the word אסור *assour*, signifies all that which is *bound*, *obliged* and *subject to rules*. אסירת *a college, a convention*, a thing which receives or which gives certain laws in certain circumstances. This is the origin of the second *Masorah*. This latter does not invent the vowel points; but it fixes the manner of using them; it treats of everything which pertains to the rules that regulate the orthography as well as the reading of the Sepher. These *Masorites* enter, as I have said, into the minutest details of the division of the chapters, and the number of verses, words and letters which compose them. They know, for example, that in the first book of the Sepher called *Berœshith*, the *Parshioth*, or great sections, are twelve in number; those named *Sedarim* or orders, forty-three in number; that there are in all one thousand five hundred and thirty-four verses, twenty thousand seven hundred and thirteen words, seventy-eight thousand, one hundred letters; and finally, that the middle of this book is at chapter 27, v. 40, at the centre of these words: וְעַל חַרְבְּךָ תִחְיֶה "And by thy sword (extermination) shalt thou live."

* I render it by *gh* or *wh*.

[7] Priscian L. I.

speaking, belonged to the same primitive stock, became by this slow revolution a kind of body, if not dead, at least in a state of lethargy wherein remained only a vague, transitory spirit giving forth only uncertain lights. At this time the meaning of the words tended to be materialized like the sound of the vowels and few of the readers were capable of grasping it. New ideas changed the meaning as new habits had changed the form.

Nevertheless, certain sages among the Assyrians, called Chaldeans, a lettered and savant caste which has been inappropriately confused with the corps of the nations;* certain Chaldean sages, I say, having perceived the successive change which had taken place in their tongue, and fearing justly that notwithstanding the oral tradition which they strove to transmit from one to the other, the meaning of the ancient books would become lost entirely, they sought a means to fix the value of the vocal characters, and particularly to give to the implied consonantal vowel, a determined sound which would prevent the word from fluctuating at hazard among several significations.

For it had come to pass that at the same time that the mother vowels, that is to say, those which were designated by the written characters, had become consonantal, the consonants, so to speak, had become vocalized by means of the vague vowel which united them. The

* The Chaldeans were not a corps of the nations, as has been ridiculously believed; but a corps of savants in a nation. Their principal academies were at Babylon, Borseppa, Sippara, Orchoe, etc. Chaldea was not, properly speaking, the name of a country, but an epithet given to the country where the Chaldeans flourished. These sages were divided into four classes, under the direction of a supreme chief. They bore, in general, the name of כשראין, *Chashdain* or of כלראין, *Chaldain*, according to the different dialects. Both of these names signified alike, *the venerables, the eminent ones, those who understand the nature of things.* They are formed of the assimilative article ל, and the words שדי or חלד which have reference to excellence, to eminence, to infinite time and to eternal nature.

many ideas which were successively attached to the same root, had brought about a concourse of vowels that it was no longer possible to blend as formerly with the spoken language, and as the written language afforded no assistance in this regard, the books became from day to day more difficult to understand.

I beg the readers but little familiar with the tongues of the Orient, to permit me to draw an example from the French. Let us suppose that we have in this tongue, a root composed of two consonants *bl*, to which we attach an idea of roundness. If we conceive trifling objects under this form, we say indifferently *bal, bel, bil, bol, bul, boul;* but in proportion as we distinguish the individuals from the species in general, we would know that a *bale* is neither a *bille,* nor a *boule;* we would be careful not to confuse the *bol* of an apothecary, with the *bôl* which is used for liquors, nor the *bill* of the English parliament with a *bulle* of the pope; in short, we make a great difference between this last *bulle* and a *bulle* of soap and a *balle* of merchandize, etc.

Now it is in this manner that the Chaldeans thought to obviate the ever growing confusion which was born of the deviation of the mother vowels and of the fixation of the vague vowels. They invented a certain number of small accents, called today vowel points, by means of which they were able to give to the characters of the alphabet under which they placed them, the sound that these characters had in the spoken language. This invention, quite ingenious, had the double advantage of preserving the writing of the ancient books, without working any change in the arrangement of the literal characters, and of permitting the noting of its pronunciation such as usage had introduced.

Here is the form, value and name of these points, which I have placed under the consonant ב solely for the purpose of serving as example; for these points can be placed under all the literal characters, consonants as well as vowels.

Long Vowels	Short Vowels
בָּ bâ—*kametz*	בַּ ba—*patah*
בֵּ bê—*zere*	בֶּ be—*segol*
בִּ bî—*hirek*	בֻּ bu—*kibbuz*
בֹּ bô—*holem*	בָּ bo—*kamez-hatef*

The point named *shewa*, represented by two points placed perpendicularly under a character, in this manner בְּ, signifies that the character under which it is placed lacks the vowel, if it is a consonant, or remains mute if it is a vowel.

The consonant שׁ always bears a point, either at the right of the writer, שׁ, to express that it has a hissing sound as in *sh;* or at the left שׂ, to signify that it is only aspirate. This difference is of but little importance; but it is essential to remark that this point replaces on the character שׁ, the vowel point called *holem*, that is to say *o*. This vocal sound precedes the consonant שׁ when the anterior consonant lacks a vowel, as in מֹשֶׁה *moshe,* it follows it when this same consonant שׁ is initial, as in שָׁנָה *shone.*

Besides these points, whose purpose was to fix the sound of the vague vowels and to determine the vocal sound which remained inherent, or which was attached to the mother vowels either as they were by nature or as they became consonants, the Chaldeans invented still another kind of interior point, intended to give more force to the consonants or to the mother vowel, in the bosom of which it is inscribed. This point is called *dagesh,* when applied to consonants, and *mappik,* when applied to vowels. The interior point *dagesh,* is inscribed in all of the consonants except ר. It is soft in the following six, ב, ג, ד, כ, ף, ת when they are initial or preceded by the mute point called *shewa;* it is hard in all the others and even in those alluded to, when they are preceded by any vowel whatever; its effect is to double their value. Certain Hebrew grammarians declare that this point, inscribed in the bosom of the consonant פ, pronounced ordinarily *ph*, gives it the force of the simple *p;* but here their opinion is sharply contested by others who assert that the Hebrews, as well as the Arabs, have never known the articulation of our *p*. But as my object is not to teach the pronunciation of Hebrew, I shall not enter into these disputes.

Indeed it is of no importance whatever in understanding the sole Hebrew book which remains to us, to know what was the articulation attached to such or such character by the orators of Jerusalem; but rather, what was the meaning that Moses, and the ancient writers who have imitated him, gave to these characters.

Let us return to the point *mappik*. This inner point is applied to three vowels ה, ו, י, and gives them a new value. The vowel ה, is distinguished from the word, and takes an emphatic or relative meaning; the vowel ו ceases to be a consonant, and becomes the primitive vowel *ou*, and if the point is transposed above it, וֹ it takes the more audible sound of *o* or *u*. The vowel י, is distinguished from the word, even as the vowel ה, and takes an emphatic sound or becomes audible from the mute that it had been.

The diphthongs, however, are quite rare in Hebrew. Nevertheless, according to the Chaldaic pronunciation, when the pure vowels ו or י, are preceded by any vowel point, or joined together, they form real diphthongs as in the following words: עֲשָׂו *heshaou,* שֶׁלָו *shaleou,* פָּנַי *phanai* גוֹי *goi,* גלוי *galoui,* etc.

The reading of the Hebraic text which I give further on in the original, and its carefully made comparison with the transcription in modern characters, will instruct those who desire to familiarize themselves with the Hebrew characters, much more than all that I might be able to tell them now, and above all they will acquire these same characters with less *ennui.*

§ III.

EFFECTS OF THE VOWEL POINTS.

SAMARITAN TEXT.

Such was the means invented by the Chaldeans to note the pronunciation of the words without altering their characters. It is impossible, lacking monuments, to fix today even by approximation, the time of this invention; but one can without deviating from the truth, determine when it was adopted by the Hebrews. Everything leads to believe that this people, having had occasion during its long captivity in Babylon to become acquainted with the Assyrian characters and the Chaldaic punctuation, found in its midst men sufficiently enlightened to appreciate the advantage of each, and to sacrifice the pride and national prejudice which might hold them attached to their ancient characters.

To Esdras is due the principal honour; a man of great genius and uncommon constancy. It was he who, shortly after the return of the Jews to Jerusalem, revised the sacred Book of his nation, repaired the disorder brought upon it by the numerous revolutions and great calamities, and transcribed it completely in Assyrian characters. It is needless to repeat here the motives and occasion of the additions which he judged proper to make. I have spoken sufficiently of this in my Introductory Dissertation. If any fault was committed in the course of a work so considerable, the evil which resulted was slight; while the good of which it became the source was immense.

For if we possess the very work of Moses in its integrity, we owe it to the particular care of Esdras and to his bold policy. The Samaritan priests who remained obstinately attached to the ancient character, finally corrupted the original text and this is how it was done.

Since they no longer pronounced the words in the same manner, they believed the changing of the orthography immaterial, and since they were deprived of means for determining the sound of the vague vowels which were fixed, they inserted mother vowels where there were none.* These vowels whose degeneration was rapid, became consonants; these consonants were charged with new vague vowels which changed the meaning of the words, besides taking from them what had been hieroglyphic, and finally the confusion became such that they were forced, in order to understand their Book, to have recourse to a translation in the language of the time. Then all was lost for them; for the translators, whatever scruples they might have brought to bear in their work, could translate only what they understood and as they understood.

What happened, however, to the rabbis of the Jewish synagogue? Thanks to the flexibility of the Chaldaic punctuation, they were able to follow the vicissitudes of

---

*Only a glance at the Samaritan text is sufficient to see that it abounds in the added mother vowels. Father Morin and Richard Simon have already remarked this: but neither has perceived how this text could in that way lose its authenticity. On the contrary, Morin pretended to draw from this abundance of mother vowels, a proof of the anteriority of the Samaritan text. He was ignorant of the fact that the greater part of the mother vowels which are lacking in the Hebraic words, are lacking designedly and that this want adds often an hieroglyphic meaning to the spoken meaning, according to the Egyptian usage. I know well that, particularly in the verbs, the copyists prior to Esdras, and perhaps Esdras himself, have neglected the mother vowels without other reason than that of following a defective pronunciation, or through indolence; but it was an inevitable misfortune. The Masorites of Tiberias may also have followed bad rules, in fixing definitely the number of these vowels. One ought in this case to supply them in reading, and an intelligent person will do so.

the pronunciation without changing anything in the substance, number or arrangement of the characters. Whereas the greater part yielding to the proneness of their gross ideas, lost as had the Samaritans, the real meaning of the sacred text; this text remained entirely concealed in its characters, the knowledge of which was preserved by an oral tradition. This tradition called Kabbala, was especially the portion of the Essenes who communicated it secretly to the initiates, neglecting the points or suppressing them wholly.

This has been the fate of the Sepher of Moses. This precious Book more and more disfigured from age to age, at first by the degeneration of the tongue, afterward by its total loss, given over to the carelessness of the ministers of the altars, to the ignorance of the people, to the inevitable digressions of the Chaldaic punctuation, was preserved by its characters which like so many of the hieroglyphics have carried the meaning to posterity. All of those whom the synagogue has considered as enlightened men, all of those whom the Christian church itself has regarded as true savants, the sages of all the centuries, have felt this truth.

Therefore, let us leave to the Hebraist grammarians the minute and ridiculous care of learning seriously and at length, the rules, wholly arbitrary, which follow the vowel points in their mutations. Let us receive these points in the Hebraic tongue, as we receive the vowels which enter in the composition of the words of other tongues without concerning ourselves as to their origin or their position. Let us not seek, as I have already said, to speak Hebrew, but to understand it. Whether such or such word is pronounced in such or such fashion in the synagogue, matters not to us. The essential thing is to know what it signifies. Let us also leave the musical notes which the rabbis call the accents, and without disturbing ourselves as to the tones in which the first chapters of the Sepher were cantillated at Jerusalem, let us consider what profound meaning was attached to it by Moses, and with that object let us seek to penetrate the inner genius of the Egyptian idiom which he has employed under its two relations, literal and hieroglyphic. We shall attain this easily by the exploration of the roots, few in number, which serve as the basis of this idiom and by an understanding of the characters, still fewer in number, which are as their elements.

For, even in the richest tongues, the roots are few in number. The Chinese tongue, one of the most varied in the whole earth, which counts eighty-four thousand characters, has scarcely more than two hundred or two hundred and thirty roots, which produce at the most, twelve or thirteen hundred simple words by variations of the accent.

CHAPTER III.

CHARACTERS CONSIDERED AS SIGNS.

§ I.

TRACED CHARACTERS, ONE OF THE ELEMENTS OF LANGUAGE:

HIEROGLYPHIC PRINCIPLE OF THEIR PRIMITIVE FORM.

We are about to examine the alphabetical form and value of the Hebrew characters; let us fix our attention now upon the meaning which is therein contained. This is a matter somewhat novel and I believe it has not been properly investigated.

According to Court de Gébelin, the origin of speech is divine. God alone can give to man the organs which are necessary for speaking; He alone can inspire in him the desire to profit by his organs; He alone can establish between speech and that multitude of marvelous objects which it must depict, that admirable *rapport* which animates speech, which makes it intelligible to all, which makes it a picture with an energy and truthfulness that cannot be mistaken. This estimable writer says, "How could one fail to recognize here the finger of the All Powerful? how could one imagine that words had no energy by themselves? that they had no value which was not conventional and which might not always be different; that the name of lamb might be that of wolf, and the name of vice that of virtue, etc."[1]

[1] *Monde primi. Orig. du lang.* p. 66.

Indeed a person must be the slave of system, and singularly ignorant of the first elements of language to assert with Hobbes and his followers, that there is nothing which may not be arbitrary in the institution of speech;[2] that "we cannot from experience conclude that anything is to be called just or unjust, true or false, or any proposition universal whatsoever, except it be from remembrance of the use of names imposed arbitrarily by men."[3]

Again if Hobbes, or those who have followed him, having delved deeply in the elements of speech, had demonstrated the nothingness or absolute indifference of it by a rational analysis of tongues or even simply by the analysis of the tongue that they spoke; but these men, compilers of certain Latin words, believed themselves so wise that the mere declaration of their paradox was its demonstration. They did not suspect that one could raise his grammatical thoughts above a supine or a gerund.

May I be pardoned for this digression which, distant as it appears from the Hebraic grammar, brings us, however, back to it; for it is in this grammar that we shall find the consoling proof, stated above by Gébelin and the response to the destructive paradoxes of Hobbes and all his acolytes. It is even one of the motives which has caused me to publish this grammar, and which, being connected with that of giving to my translation of the Cosmogony of Moses an incontrovertible basis, engages me in a work to which I had not at first destined myself.

I shall show that the words which compose the tongues in general, and those of the Hebraic tongue in particular, far from being thrown at hazard, and formed by the explosion of an arbitrary caprice, as has been asserted, are, on the contrary, produced by a profound reason. I shall prove that there is not a single one that may not, by means of a well made grammatical analysis

[2] Hobb. *de la nat. hum.* ch. 4. 10.
[3] *Ibid*: ch. 5. § 10. **Leviath**. ch. 4.

be brought back to the fixed elements of a nature, immutable as to substance, although variable to infinity as to forms.

These elements, such as we are able to examine here, constitute that part of speech to which I have given the name of *sign*. They comprise, as I have said, the voice, the gesture, and the traced characters. It is to the traced characters that we shall apply ourselves; since the voice is extinct, and the gesture disappeared. They alone will furnish us a subject amply vast for reflections.

According to the able writer whom I have already quoted, their form is by no means arbitrary. Court de Gébelin proves by numerous examples that the first inventors of the literal alphabet, unique source of all the literal alphabets in actual use upon the earth, and whose characters were at first only sixteen in number, drew from nature itself the form of these characters, relative to the meaning which they wished to attach to them. Here are his ideas upon this subject, to which I shall bring only some slight changes and certain developments necessitated by the extent of the Hebraic alphabet and the comparison that I am obliged to make of several analogous letters; in order to reduce the number to the sixteen primordial characters, and make them harmonize with their hieroglyphic principle.

א   A.—Man himself as collective unity, principle: master and ruler of the earth.

ב פ   B. P. PH.—The mouth of man as organ of speech; his interior, his habitation, every central object.

כ ג   G. C. CH.—The throat: the hand of man half closed and in action of taking: every canal, every enclosure, every hollow object.

ת ד   D. DH. TH.—The breast: every abundant, nutritive object: all division, all reciprocity.

ה   H. EH. AH.—The breath: all that which animates: air, life, being.

ו O. U.—The eye: all that which is related to the light, to brilliancy, to limpidness, to water.

עון OU. W. WH.—The ear: all that which is related to sound, to noise, to wind: void, nothingness.

שסן Z. S. SH.—A staff, an arrow, a bow; the arms, the instruments of man: every object leading to an end.

ח H. HE. CH.—A field, image of natural existence: all that which requires work, labour, effort: all that which excites heat.

ט צ T. TZ.—A roof: a place of surety, of refuge: a haven, a shelter; a term, an aim: an end.

י I.—The finger of man, his extended hand: all that which indicates the directing power and which serves to manifest it.

ל L.—The arm: everything which is extended, raised, displayed.

מ M.—The companion of man, woman: all that which is fruitful and creative.

נ N.—The production of woman: a child: any fruit whatsoever: every produced being.

ק Q. K.—A positive arm: all that which serves, defends, or makes an effort for man.

ר R.—The head of man: all that which possesses in itself, a proper and determining movement.

Now it must be observed that these characters received these symbolic figures from their first inventors only because they already contained the idea; that in passing to the state of signs, they present only abstractly to the thought the faculties of these same objects: but, as I have stated, they can fulfill the functions of the *signs*, only after having been veritable *nouns*: for every *sign* manifested exteriorly is at first a *noun*.

§ II.

ORIGIN OF SIGNS AND THEIR DEVELOPMENT:

THOSE OF THE HEBRAIC TONGUE.

Let us try to discover how the *sign*, being manifested exteriorly, produced a *noun*, and how the *noun*, characterized by a figured type produced a *sign*. Let us take for example, the sign מ M, which, expressing by means of its primordial elements, the sound and organs of the voice, becomes the syllable aM or Ma, and is applied to those faculties of woman which eminently distinguish her, that is to say, to those of mother. If certain minds attacked by skepticism ask me why I restrict the idea of mother in this syllable aM or Ma, and how I am sure that it is applied effectively there, I shall reply to them that the sole proof that I can give them, in the material sphere which envelops them is, that in all the tongues of the world from that of the Chinese to that of the Caribs, the syllable aM or Ma is attached to the idea of mother, and aB, Ba, or aP, Pa, to that of father. If they doubt my assertion let them prove that it is false; if they do not doubt it, let them tell me how it is that so many diverse peoples, thrown at such distances apart, unknown to each other, are agreed in the signification of this syllable, if this syllable is not the innate expression of the sign of maternity.

This is a grammatical truth that all the sophisms of Hobbes and his disciples knew not how to overthrow.

Let us settle upon this fundamental point and proceed. What are the relative or abstract ideas which are attached to, or which follow from, the primordial idea represented by the syllable aM or Ma? Is it not the idea of fecundity, of multiplicity, of abundance? Is it not the idea of fecundation, of multiplication, of formation? Does not one see from this source, every idea of excited and passive action, of exterior movement, of plastic force, of characteristic place, of home, of means, etc?

It is useless to pursue this examination: the mass of ideas contained in the primordial idea of mother, is either attached to the figured sign, to the typical character which represents it, or is derived from and follows it.

Each *sign* starts from the same principles and acquires the same development. Speech is like a sturdy tree which, shooting up from a single trunk begins with a few branches; but which soon extends itself, spreads, and becomes divided in an infinity of boughs whose interlaced twigs are blended and mingled together.

And do not wonder at this immense number of ideas following from so small a number of *signs*. It is by means of the eight keys called *Koua*, that the Chinese tongue, at first reduced to two hundred and forty primordial characters, is raised to eighty and even eighty-four thousand derivative characters, as I have already said.

Now the newer a tongue is and closer to nature, the more the *sign* preserves its force. This force dies out insensibly, in proportion as the derivative tongues are formed, blended, identified and mutually enriched with a mass of words which, belonging to several tribes at first isolated and afterward united, lose their synonymy and finally are coloured with all the nuances of the imagination, and adapt themselves to every delicacy of sentiment and expression. The force of the *sign* is the grammatical touchstone by means of which one can judge without error the antiquity of any tongue.

In our modern tongues, for example, the *sign*, because of the idiomatic changes brought about by time, is very difficult to recognize; it yields only to a persistent analysis. It is not thus in Hebrew. This tongue, like a vigorous shoot sprung from the dried trunk of the pri-

ORIGIN OF SIGNS OF HEBRAIC TONGUE

mitive tongue, has preserved on a small scale all the forms and all the action. The *signs* are nearly all evident, and many even are detached: when this is the case, I shall give them name of *relations* for I understand by *sign* only the constitutive character of a root, or the character which placed at the beginning or at the end of a word, modifies its expression without conserving any in itself.

I now pass, after these explanations, to what the Hebraic *signs* indicate, that is to say, to a new development of the literal characters of the Hebraic tongue considered under the relation of the primitive ideas which they express, and by which they are constituted representative *signs* of these same ideas.

א A.—This first character of the alphabet, in nearly all known idioms, is the sign of power and of stability. The ideas that it expresses are those of unity and of the principle by which it is determined.

ב B. P.—Virile and paternal sign: image of active and interior action.

ג G.—This character which offers the image of a canal, is the organic sign; that of the material covering and of all ideas originating from the corporeal organs or from their action.

ד D.—Sign of nature, divisible and divided: it expresses every idea proceeding from the abundance born of division.

ה H. He.—Life and every abstract idea of being.

ו OU. W.—This character offers the image of the most profound, the most inconceivable mystery, the image of the knot which unites, or the point which separates nothingness and being. It is the universal, convertible sign which makes a thing pass from one nature to another; communicating on the one side, with the sign of light and of spiritual sense ו, which is itself more elevated, and connecting on the other side, in its degeneration, with the sign of darkness and of material sense ע which is itself still more abased.

ז Z. C. S.—Demonstrative sign: abstract image of the link which unites things: symbol of luminous refraction.

ח H. HE. CH.—This character, intermediary between ה and כ, the former designating life, absolute existence; the latter, relative life, assimilated existence. —is the sign of elementary existence: it offers the image of a sort of equilibrium, and is attached to ideas of effort, of labour, and of normal and of legislative action.

ט T.—Sign of resistance and of protection. This character serves as link between ד and ת, which are both much more expressive.

י I.—Image of potential manifestation: of spiritual duration, of eternity of time and of all ideas relating thereunto: remarkable character in its vocal nature, but which loses all of its faculties in passing to the state of consonant, wherein it depicts no more than a material duration, a sort of link as ו, or of movement as שׁ.

כ C. CH.—Assimilative sign: it is a reflective and transient life, a sort of mould which receives and makes all forms. It is derived from the character ח which proceeds itself from the sign of absolute life ה. Thus holding, on the one side, to elementary life, it joins to the signification of the character ח, that of the organic sign ג, of which it is, besides, only a kind of reinforcement.

ל L.—Sign of expansive movement: it is applied to all

ORIGIN OF SIGNS OF HEBRAIC TONGUE

ideas of extension, elevation, occupation, possession. As final sign, it is the image of power derived from elevation.

מ **M.**—Maternal and female sign: local and plastic sign: image of exterior and passive action. This character used at the end of words, becomes the collective sign ם. In this state, it develops the being in indefinite space, or it comprises, in the same respect, all beings of an identical nature.

נ **N.**—Image of produced or reflected being: sign of individual and of corporeal existence. As final character it is the augmentative sign ן, and gives to the word which receives it all the individual extension of which the expressed thing is susceptible.

ס **S. X.**—Image of all circumscription: sign of circular movement in that which has connection with its circumferential limit. It is the link ו reinforced and turned back upon itself.

ע **H. WH.**—Sign of material meaning. It is the sign ו considered in its purely physical relations. When the vocal sound ע, degenerates in its turn into consonant, it becomes the sign of all that which is bent, false, perverse and bad.

פ **PH. F.**—Sign of speech and of that which is related to it. This character serves as link between the characters ב and ו, B and V, when the latter has passed into state of consonant; it participates in all their significations, adding its own expression which is the emphasis.

צ **TZ.**—Final and terminative sign being related to all ideas of scission, of term, solution, goal. Placed at the beginning of words, it indicates the movement which carries toward the term of which it is the sign: placed at the end, it marks the same term where it has tended; then it receives this form ץ, It is derived from the character ם and from the character ז, and it marks equally scission for both.

ק Q. K.—Sign eminently compressive, astringent and trenchant; image of the agglomerating or repressive form. It is the character כ wholly materialized and is applied to objects purely physical. For this is the progression of the signs: ה, universal life; ח, elementary existence, the effort of nature; כ, assimilated life holding the natural forms; ק material existence giving the means of forms.

ר R.—Sign of all movement proper, good or bad: original and frequentative sign: image of the renewal of things as to their movement.

ש SH.—Sign of relative duration and of movement therewith connected. This character is derived from the vocal sound י, passed into the state of consonant; it joins to its original expression the respective significations of the characters ז and ם.

ת TH.—Sign of reciprocity: image of that which is mutual and reciprocal. Sign of signs. Joining to the abundance of the character ר, to the force of the resistance and protection of the character ש, the idea of perfection of which it is itself the symbol.

Twenty-two signs: such are the simple bases upon which reposes the Hebraic tongue, upon which are raised the primitive or derivative tongues which are attached to the same origin. From the perfect understanding of these bases, depends the understanding of their genius: their possession is a key which unlocks the roots.

§ III.

USE OF THE SIGNS: EXAMPLE DRAWN FROM THE FRENCH.

I might expatiate at length upon the signification of each of these characters considered as *Signs*. especially if I had added to the general ideas that they express, some of the particular, relative or abstract ideas which are necessarily attached; but I have said enough for the attentive reader and he will find elsewhere in the course of this work quite a considerable number of examples and developments to assure his progress and level all doubts which he might have conceived.

As I have not yet spoken of the *noun,* fundamental part of speech, and as it would be difficult for those of my readers, who have of the Hebraic tongue only the knowledge that I am giving them, to understand me if I proceeded abruptly to the composition or the decomposition of the Hebraic words by means of the sign, I shall put off demonstrating the form and utility of this labour. In order, however, not to leave this chapter imperfect and to satisfy the curiosity as much as possible, without fatiguing too much the attention, I shall illustrate the power of the sign by a French word, taken at hazard, of a common acceptation and of obvious composition.

Let it be the word *emplacement.** Only a very super-

---

* At the very moment of writing this, I was at the *Bureau des Opérations militaires du Ministère de la guerre*, where I was then employed. Just as I was seeking for the French word announced in the above paragraph, the chief of the division interrupted me, in order to give me some work to do relative to an *emplacement* of troops. My administrative labour terminated, I again took up my grammatical work, retaining the same word which had engaged my attention.

ficial knowledge of etymology is necessary to see that the simple word here is *place*. Our first task is to connect it with the tongue from which it is directly derived; by this means we shall obtain an etymology of the first degree, which will set to rights the changes which might be effected in the characters of which it is composed. Now, whether we go to the Latin tongue, or whether we go to the Teutonic tongue, we shall find in the one *platea*, and in the other *platz*. We shall stop there without seeking the etymology of the second degree, which would consist in interrogating the primitive Celt, common origin of the Latin and the Teutonic; because the two words that we have obtained suffice to enlighten us.

It is evident that the constitutive root of the French word *place*, is *aT* or *aTz*. Now, the sign in *at*, indicates to us an idea of resistance or of protection, and in *atz* an idea of term, of limit, of end. It is, therefore, a thing resisting and limited, or a thing protective and final. But what is the sign which governs this root and which makes it a noun, by proceeding from right to left following the Oriental manner? It is the sign L, that of all extension, of all possession. *Lat* is therefore, a thing extended as *læt,* or extended and possessed as *latitude*. This is unimpeachable.

Next, what is the second sign which stamps a new meaning on these words? It is the sign P, that of active and central action; inner and determinative character; which, from the word *læt*, an extended thing, makes a thing of a fixed and determined extent, a *plat*, or a *place* by changing the *t* into *c*, as the etymology of the first degree has proved to us the reality of this change.

Now that we understand clearly in the word *em-placement*, the simple word *place* of which it is composed, let us search for the elements of its composition. Let us examine first the termination *ment*, a kind of adverbial relation, which added to a noun, determines, in French, an action implied. The etymology of the first degree gives us *mens,* in Latin, and *mind* in Teutonic. These two words mutually explain each other, therefore it is unnecessary for us to turn to the second degree of etymology. Whether we take *mens* or *mind,* it remains for us to explore the root *eN* or *iN,* after dropping the initial character M, and the final S or D, that we shall take up further on. To the root *en,* expressing something even in the tongue of the Latins, we shall now direct our attention.

Here we see the sign of absolute life E, and that of reflective or produced existence N, joined together to designate every particular being. This is precisely what the Latin root EN, signfies, *lo, behold;* that is to say, *see; examine* this individual existence. It is the exact translation of the Hebrew הן *hen!* If you add to this root the luminous sign as in the Greek αἰών (*æon*), you will have the individual being nearest to the absolute being; if, on the contrary, you take away the sign of life and substitute that of duration as in the Latin *in,* you will have the most restricted, the most centralized, the most interior being.

But let the root EN be terminated by the conscriptive and circumferential sign S, and we shall obtain *ens,* corporeal mind, the intelligence peculiar to man. Then let us make this word rule by the exterior and plastic sign M, and we shall have the word *mens,* intelligence manifesting itself outwardly and producing. This is the origin of the termination sought for: it expresses the exterior form according to which every action is modified.

As to the initial syllable *em,* which is found at the head of the word *em-place-ment,* it represents the root EN, and has received the character M, only because of the consonant P, which never allows N in front of it, and this, as though the being generated could never be presented prior to the generating being. This syllable comes therefore from the same source, and whether it be derived from the corresponding Latin words *en* or *in,* it always characterizes restricted existence in a determined or inner point.

According to these ideas, if I had to explain the French word *em-place-ment*, I would say that it signifies the proper mode according to which a fixed and determined extent, as *place*, is conceived or is presented exteriorly.

Moreover, this use of the sign which I have just illustrated by a word of the French tongue, is much easier and more sure in the Hebrew, which, possessing in itself nearly all the constitutive elements, only obliges the etymologist on very rare occasions to leave his lexicon; whereas, one cannot analyze a French word without going back to Latin or Teutonic, from which it is derived, and without making frequent incursions into Celtic, its primitive source, and into Greek and Phœnician, from which it has received at different times a great number of expressions.

CHAPTER IV.

THE SIGN PRODUCING THE ROOT.

§ I.

DIGRESSION ON THE PRINCIPLE AND THE CONSTITUTIVE ELEMENTS OF THE SIGN.

I have endeavoured to show in the preceding chapter, the origin of the sign and its power: let us again stop a moment upon this important subject, and though I might be accused of lacking method, let us not fear to retrace our steps, the better to assure our progress.

I have designated as elements of speech, the voice, the gesture and the traced characters; as means, the sound, the movement and the light: but these elements and these means would exist in vain, if there were not at the same time a creative power, independent of them, which could take possession of them and put them into action. This power is the Will. I refrain from naming its principle; for besides being difficult to conceive, it would not be the place here to speak of it. But the existence of the will cannot be denied even by the most determined skeptic; since he would be unable to call it in question without willing it and consequently without giving it recognition.

Now the articulate voice and the affirmative or negative gesture are, and can only be, the expression of the will. It is the will which, taking possession of sound and movement, forces them to become its interpreters and to reflect exteriorly its interior affections.

Nevertheless, if the will is absolute, all its affections although diverse, must be identical; that is to say, be respectively the same for all individuals who experience them. Thus, a man willing and affirming his will by gesture or vocal inflection, experiences no other affection than any man who wills and affirms the same thing. The gesture and sound of the voice which accompany the affirmation are not those destined to depict negation, and there is not a single man on earth who can not be made to understand by the gesture or by the inflection of the voice, that he is loved or that he is hated; that he wishes or does not wish the thing presented. There would be nothing of agreement here. It is an identical power which is manifested spontaneously and which radiating from one volitive centre reflects itself upon the other.

I would it were as easy to demonstrate that it is equally without agreement and by the sole force of the will, that the gesture or vocal inflection assigned to affirmation or negation is transformed into different words, and how it happens, for example, that the words לא, *no*, and כה, *yes*, having the same sound and involving the same inflection and the same gesture, have not, however, the same meaning; but if that were so easy, how has the origin of speech remained till now unknown? How is it that so many savants armed with both synthesis and analysis, have not solved a question so important to man? There is nothing conventional in speech, and I hope to prove this to my readers; but I do not promise to prove to them, a truth of this nature in the manner of the geometricians; its possession is of too high an importance to be contained in an algebraic equation.

Let us return. Sound and movement placed at the disposition of the will is modified by it; that is to say, that by certain appropriate organs, sound is articulated and changed into voice; movement is determined and changed into gesture. But voice and gesture have only an instantaneous, fugitive duration. If it is of importance to the will of man, to make the memory of the affections that it manifests exteriorly survive the affections themselves (for this is nearly always of importance to him); then,

THE SIGN PRODUCING THE ROOT

finding no resource to fix or to depict the sound, it takes possession of movement and with the aid of the hand, its most expressive organ, finds after many efforts, the secret of drawing on the bark of trees or cutting on stone, the gesture upon which it has at first determined. This is the origin of traced characters which, as image of the gesture and symbol of the vocal inflection, become one of the most fruitful elements of language, which extend its empire rapidly and present to man an inexhaustible means of combination. There is nothing conventional in their principle; for *no* is always *no,* and *yes* always *yes:* a man is a man. But as their form depends much upon the designer who first tests the will by depicting his affections, enough of the arbitrary can be insinuated, and it can be varied enough so that there may be need of an agreement to assure their authenticity and authorize their usage. Also, it is always in the midst of a tribe advanced in civilization and subject to the laws of a regular government, that the use of some kind of writing is encountered. One can be sure that wherever traced characters are found, there also are found civilized forms. All men, however savage they may be, speak and impart to each other their ideas; but all do not write, because there is no need of agreement for the establishment of a language, whereas there is always need of one for writing.

Nevertheless, although traced characters infer an agreement, as I have already said, it must not be forgotten that they are the symbol of two things which are not inferred, the vocal inflection and the gesture. These are the result of the spontaneous outburst of the will. The others are the fruit of reflection. In tongues similar to Hebrew, where the vocal inflection and the gesture have long since disappeared, one must devote himself to the characters, as the sole element which remains of the language, and regard them as the complete language itself, not considering the agreement by which they have been established. This is what I have done, in constituting them representative signs of the fundamental ideas of the Hebraic tongue. I shall follow the same method showing successively how this small quantity of signs has sufficed for the formation of the roots of this tongue, and for the composition of all the words which have been derived therefrom. Let us examine first what I mean by a root.

§ II.

FORMATION OF THE ROOT AND OF THE RELATION.

A root is, and can never be anything but, monosyllabic: it results from the union of two signs at the least, and of three at the most. I say two signs at the least, for a single sign cannot constitute a root, because the fundamental idea that it contains, being, as it were, only in germ, awaits the influence of another sign in order to be developed. It is not that the sign before being constituted such, may not have represented a noun, but this noun becomes effaced, as I have said, to constitute the sign. When the sign is presented alone in speech, it becomes, in Hebrew, what I call an article; that is to say, a sort of relation whose expression entirely abstract, determines the diverse relations of nouns and verbs to each other.

The root cannot be composed of more than three signs, without being dissyllabic and consequently without ceasing to be of the number of primitive words. Every word composed of more than one syllable is necessarily a derivative. For, two roots are either united or contracted; or else one or several signs have been joined to the radical root for its modification.

Although the etymological root may be very well employed as noun, verb or relation, all that, however, does not matter, so long as one considers it as root; seeing that it offers in this respect no determined idea of object, action or abstraction. A noun designates openly a particular object of whatever nature it may be, a verb expresses some sort of action, a relation determines a *rapport:* the root presents always a meaning universal as noun, absolute as verb, and indeterminate as relation.

Thus the root אִי, formed of the signs of power and of manifestation, designates, in general, the centre toward which the will tends, the place where it is fixed, its sphere of activity. Employed as noun, it is a desire, a desired object: a place distinct and separate from another place; an isle, a country, a region, a home, a government: as verb, it is the action of desiring a thing eagerly, of tending toward a place, of delighting therein: as relation, it is the abstract connection of the place where one is, of the object to which one tends, of the sphere wherein one acts.

Thus the root אוֹ, which unites to the sign of power, the universal, convertible sign, image of the mysterious knot which brings nothingness to being, offers even a vaguer meaning than the root אִי, of which I have spoken, and of which it seems to be a modification. Nor is it yet a desire, even in general; it is, so to speak, the germ of a desire, a vague appetence, without aim and without object; a desirous uneasiness, an obtuse sense. Employed as noun, it designates the uncertainty of the will; if it is made a verb, it is the indeterminate action of willing; if it is used as relation, it is the abstract expression of the affinity that the uncertainty or indetermination of the will, establishes between one or the other object which attracts it. This root, considered rightly as primitive, produces a great number of derivative roots by becoming amalgamated with other primitive roots, or receiving them by the adjunction of the signs which modify it. One finds, for example, the following, which are worthy of closest attention.

אוֹב All desire acting inwardly and fructifying. It is, as noun, the matrix of the Universe, the vessel of Isis, the Orphic egg, the World, the Pythonic spirit; etc.

אוֹד Every desire acting outwardly and being propagated. As noun, it is that which binds cause to effect, the causality; any sort of emanation; as verb, it is the action of emanating, of passing from cause to effect; as relation, it is the abstract affinity according to which one conceives that a thing exists, or takes place *because* of another.

אֻל Every expansive desire being projected into space. As noun, it is an interval of time or place; a duration, a distance; as verb, it is the action of being extended, of filling, of invading time or space; that of waiting or lasting; as relation, it is the abstract affinity expressed by *perhaps*.

און Every desire spreading into infinity, losing itself in vacuity, vanishing: as noun, it is everything and nothing according to the manner in which one considers infinity.

אף Every desire subjugating another and drawing it into its vortex: as noun, it is the sympathetic force, the passion; a final cause: as verb, it is the action of drawing into its will, of enveloping in its vortex: as relation, it is the abstract affinity expressed by *same, likewise*.

אץ Every desire leading to a goal. As noun, it is the very limit of desire, the end to which it tends; as verb, it is the action of pushing, of hastening, of pressing toward the desired object: as relation, it is the abstract affinity expressed by *at*.

אור Every desire given over to its own impulse. As noun, it is ardour, fire, passion: as verb, it is that which embraces, burns, excites, literally as well as figuratively.

אות All sympathizing desire; being in accord with another. As noun it is a symbol, a character, any object whatever: as verb, it is the action of sympathizing, of being in accord with, of agreeing, of being *en rapport*, in harmony; as relation it is the abstract affinity expressed by *together*.

I shall give no more examples on this subject since my plan is to give, in the course of this Grammar, a series of all the Hebraic roots. It is there that I invite the reader to study their form. I shall be careful to distinguish the primitive roots from the compound, intensive or onomatopoetic roots. Those of the latter kind are quite rare in

Hebrew. One finds them in much greater numbers in Arabic where many local circumstances have called them into existence. This concurrence of imitative sounds, very favourable to poetry and to all the arts of imitation, must have been greatly prejudicial to the development of universal ideas toward which the Egyptians directed their greatest efforts.

It is an unfortunate mistake to imagine that the examination of Hebraic roots is as difficult as it is in the modern idioms. In these idioms, raised, for the most part, upon the *débris* of many united idioms, the roots deeply buried beneath the primitive materials, can deceive the eye of the observer; but it cannot do thus in Hebrew. This tongue, thanks to the form of the Chaldaic characters which have changed scarcely anything but its punctuation, offers still to an observant reader who does not wish to concern himself with the vowel points, the terms used by Moses in their native integrity. If, notwithstanding the precautions of Esdras, there have crept in certain alterations in the mother vowels and even in the consonants, these alterations are slight and do not prevent the root, nearly level with the ground, if I may thus express it, from striking the eye of the etymologist.

Let us examine now what I mean by the relations.

The relations are, as I have said, extracted by thought from the signs, nouns or verbs. They express always a connection of the sign with the noun, of the noun with the noun, or of the noun with the verb. Thence, the simple and natural division which I establish, in three kinds, according to the part of speech with which they preserve the greatest analogy. I call designative relation or *article*, that which marks the connection of the sign with the noun: nominal relation or *pronoun*, that which indicates the connection of the noun with the noun, or of the noun with the verb; and finally adverbial relation or *adverb*. that which characterizes the connection of the verb with the verb, or of the verb with the noun. I use here these

FORMATION OF ROOT AND RELATION

denominations known as article, pronoun and adverb to avoid prolixity; but without admitting in Hebrew the distinctions or the definitions that grammarians have admitted in other tongues.

The relations, forming together a kind of grammatical bond which circulates among the principal parts of speech, must be considered separately, kind by kind, and according as they are connected with the sign, noun or verb. I am about to speak of the designative relation or article, since I have already made known the sign: but I shall put off speaking of the nominal relation, because I have already spoken of the noun, and shall deal later with the adverbial relation having already dealt with the verb.

The designative relation or article, is represented under three headings in the Hebraic tongue, namely: under that of the relation properly speaking, or *article*, of the prepositive relation, or *preposition*. and of the interjective relation, or *interjection*. The article differs principally from the sign, by what it preserves of its own peculiar force, and by what it communicates to the noun to which it is joined; a sort of movement which changes nothing of the primitive signification of this noun; nevertheless it is strictly united there and is composed of but one single character.

I enumerate six articles in Hebrew, without including the designative preposition את, of which I shall speak later. They have neither gender nor number. The following are the articles with the kind of movement that they express.

ה DETERMINATIVE ARTICLE.—It determines the noun; that is to say, that it draws the object which it designates from a mass of similar objects and gives it a local existence. Derived from the sign ה, which contains the idea of universal life, it presents itself under several acceptations as article. By the first, it points out simply the noun that it modifies and is rendered by the corresponding articles *the; this, that, these, those:*

by the second, it expresses a relation of dependence or division, and is translated *of the; of this, of that, of these, of those:* by the third, it adds to the noun before which it is placed, only an emphatic meaning, a sort of exclamatory accent. In this last acceptation, it is placed indifferently at the beginning or at the end of words and is joined with the greater part of the other articles without being harmful to their movement. Therefore I call it *Emphatic article,* and when I translate it, which I rarely do lacking means, I render it by *o! oh! ah!* or simply by the exclamation point (!).

ל DIRECTIVE ARTICLE.—It expresses, with nouns or actions whose movement it modifies, a direct relation of union, of possession, or of coincidence. I translate it by *to, at, for, according to, toward,* etc.

מ EXTRACTIVE OR PARTITIVE ARTICLE.—The movement which this article expresses, with nouns or actions that it modifies, is that by which a noun or an action is taken for the means, for the instrument, by which they are divided in their essence, or drawn from the midst of several other nouns or similar actions. I render it ordinarily by *from, out of, by; with, by means of, among, between,* etc.

ב MEDIATIVE OR INTEGRAL ARTICLE.—This article characterizes with nouns or actions, almost the same movement as the extractive article מ, but with more force, and without any extraction or division of the parts. Its analogues are: *in, by, with, while,* etc.

כ ASSIMILATIVE ARTICLE.—The movement which it expresses, with nouns or actions is that of similitude, of analogy, and of concomitance. I render it by: *as, similar; such as, according to,* etc.

ו CONJUNCTIVE OR CONVERTIBLE ARTICLE.—This article. in uniting nouns, causes the movement of nothingness, of which the character ו becomes the sign, as we have seen: in making actions pass from one time to another.

FORMATION OF ROOT AND RELATION 113

it exercises upon them the convertible faculty of which this same character is the universal emblem. Its conjunctive movement can be rendered by: *and, also, thus, then, afterward, that,* etc. But its convertible movement is not expressible in our tongue and I do not know of any in which it can be expressed. In order to perceive it one must feel the Hebraic genius.

The chapters wherein I shall treat of the noun and the verb will contain the necessary examples to illustrate the use of these six articles whether relative to the noun or the verb.

§ III.

PREPOSITION AND INTERJECTION.

Articles, which we shall now examine, remain articles, properly speaking, only so far as they are composed of a single literal character and as they are joined intimately to the noun, the verb or the relation which they govern; when they are composed of several characters and when they act apart or are simply united to words by a hyphen, I call them prepositive articles or *prepositions*: they become *interjections* when, in this state of isolation, they offer no longer any relation with the noun or the verb, and express only a movement of the mind too intense to be otherwise characterized.

Prepositions, intended to serve as link between things, and to show their respective function, lose their meaning when once separated from the noun which they modify. Interjections, on the contrary, have only as much force as they have independence. Differing but little in sound, they differ infinitely in the expression, more or less accentuated, that they receive from the sentiment which produces them. They belong, as a learned man has said, "to all time, to all places, to all peoples": they form an universal language.[1]

I am about to give here, the prepositions and interjections which are the most important to understand, so as to fix the ideas of the reader upon the use of these kinds of relations. I am beginning with those prepositions which take the place of the articles already cited.

חַא׃ *determinative prep.* replaces the article ה.
אֶל, אֱלֵי or עַל׃ *directive* " " " " ל.
מִן, מֶנֵּי or מִמֶּנִּי׃ *extractive* " " " " מ.

[1] Court de Geb: *Gramm. Univ.* p. 353.

PREPOSITION AND INTERJECTION 115

בְּ. *mediative* prep. replaces the article בִּ׳, בְּדֵי or בְּמוֹ:
כְּ. *assimilative* " " " " כִּ׳, כְּה or כְּמוֹ:

    The conjunctive and convertible article וְ is not replaceable.

אֶת, אוֹת: *designative preposition:* has **no corresponding** article.

גַם, גַם כִּי: same, also, as ⎫
כִּי: that   ⎬ *conjunctive prepositions*
עִם, עָמָד: with   ⎪
אַף: likewise, even ⎭

אוֹ: either, or ⎫
בַּל: neither, nor ⎬ *disjunctive prepositions*
בְּלִי, בִּלְתִּי, מִבְּלִי: without ⎭

אַךְ: but, except ⎫
אוּלָם: nevertheless ⎬ *restrictive prepositions*
רַק: save, at least ⎭

אִם, כִּי אִם: if, but if ⎫ *conditional prepositions*
אוּלַי: perhaps   ⎭

יוֹתֵר: besides, moreover ⎫ *additive prepositions*
מְאֹד: very, more   ⎭

אֵצֶל: near, with ⎫ *final prepositions*
עַד עֲדֵי: at, as far as ⎭

בְּעַד: for ⎫
כְּפִי, לְפִי: according to ⎪
כִּי: for, because ⎪
חֵלֶף: on account of ⎬ *discursive prepositions*
יַעַן כִּי: since ⎪
לָכֵן: therefore ⎪
עַל־כֵּן: now then, so ⎪
לְמַעַן: as ⎭
    etc., etc.,

INTERJECTIONS.

אָח, אוֹי, אוֹיָה׃	ah! woe! alas!
הָ, הָא׃	oh! heavens!
הֶאָח׃	now then! come **now**!
הָבָה׃	take care! mind!
הוֹי׃	indeed!
לוּ, אַחֲלֵי׃	would to God!
	etc., etc.,

I believe it quite useless to prolong this list and to dwell upon the particular signification of each of these relations; however, there is one of which I must speak, because its usage is very frequent in the tongue of Moses, and also because we shall see it soon figuring in the nominal inflection, and joining its movement to that of the articles. This is the designative preposition אֵת, which I have mentioned as having no corresponding article.

The movement which expresses this preposition with the nouns which it modifies, is that by which it puts them *en rapport* as governing or governed, as independent one of the other and participating in the same action. I name it *designative,* on account of the sign of signs, ת, from which it is derived. It characterizes sympathy and reciprocity when it is taken substantively. Joined to a noun by a hyphen אֶת־, it designates the substance proper and individual, the identity, the selfsameness, the seity, the *thou-ness,* if I may be permitted this word; that is to say, that which constitutes *thou,* that which implies something apart from *me,* a thing that is not *me;* in short, the presence of another substance. This important preposition, of which I cannot give the exact meaning, indicates the coincidence, the spontaneity of actions, the liaison, the *ensemble* and the dependence of things.

The designative relation that I am considering in connection with the article, preposition and interjection, will be easily distinguished from the nominal relation concerning which I shall speak later on; because this relation is not intended either to modify nouns or to set forth the confused and indeterminate movements of the mind; but serves as supplement to nouns, becomes their lieutenant, so to speak, and shows their mutual dependence. This same relation will not be, it is true, so easy to distinguish from the adverbial relation, and I admit that often one will meet with some that are, at the same time, prepositions and adverbs. But this very analogy will furnish the proof of what I have advanced, that the relation extracted by thought, from the sign, the noun and the verb, circulates among these three principal parts of speech and is modified to serve them as common bond.

One can observe, for example, that the designative relation tends to become adverbial and that it becomes thus whenever it is used in an absolute manner with the verb, or when the article is joined, making it a sort of adverbial substantive. Therefore one can judge that *upon, in, outside,* are designative relations, or prepositions when one says: *upon that; in the present; outside this point:* but one cannot mistake them for adverbials when one says: *I am above; I am within; I am without.* It is in this state that they are taken to be inflected with the article. *I see the above, the within, the without; I come from above, from within, from without; I go above, within, without;* etc. The Hebraic tongue, which has not these means of construction, makes use of the same words עַל, חוּץ, בֵּית to express equally *upon, above, the upper part; in, the inside; out, beyond, the outside.* It is to these fine points that great attention must be given in translating Moses.

As to the vowel points which accompany the different relations of which I shall speak, they vary in such a way, that it would be vainly wasting precious time to consider them here; so much the more as these variations change nothing as to the meaning, which alone concerns me, and alters only the pronunciation, which does not concern me.

I am always surprised, in reading the majority of the Grammars written upon the Hebraic tongue, to see with what scruples, with what tedious care they treat a miserable *kamez*, or a still more miserable *kamez-hatif;* whereas they hardly deign to dwell upon the meaning of the most important words. Numberless pages are found jumbled with the uncouth names of *zere, segol, patah, holem,* and not one where the sign is mentioned, not one where it is even a question of this basis, at once so simple and so fecund, both of the Hebraic language and of all the languages of the world.

CHAPTER V.

THE NOUN.

THE NOUN CONSIDERED UNDER SEVEN RELATIONS.

§ I.

ETYMOLOGY

The noun, I repeat, is the basis of speech; for, although it may be the product of the sign, the sign without it would have no meaning, and if the sign had no meaning, there would exist neither relations nor verbs.

We shall consider the nouns of the Hebraic tongue, under seven relations, namely: under the first six, of Etymology, Quality, Gender, Number, Movement and Construction, and then, under the seventh relation of Signification, which includes them all.

The Hebraist grammarians, dazzled by the *éclat* of the verb and by the extensive use of the verbal faculties, have despoiled the noun of its etymological rank to give it to the verb, thus deriving from the verb not only the equi-literal substantives, that is to say, compounds of the same number of characters, but even those which offer less: claiming, for example, that גַל *a heap*, is formed from גָלַל *he heaps up;* that אָב *father,* is derived from אָבָה *he willed;* that אֵשׁ *the fire,* finds its origin in אָשַׁשׁ *he was strong and robust,* etc.

It is needless for me to say into how many errors they have fallen by this false course, and how far distant they are from the real etymological goal. The lexicons also, of these Hebraists, all constructed after this method, are only crude vocabularies, where the simplest words, thrown more or less far from their root, according as the verb bids it, are presented almost never in their real place, or in the true light which would facilitate their comprehension.

I have spoken sufficiently of the sign and its value, of the root and its formation; I now intend to give certain simple rules to lead to the etymological understanding of the noun.

Often a *noun* properly speaking, is, in the tongue of the Hebrews, only its root used in a more restricted sense: as when uniting the idea of paternity and maternity upon a single subject, one pronounces אב, *father,* or אם *mother.* It is then a movement of the thought upon itself, which makes of a thing that it had conceived in general, a determined thing, by which it qualifies a particular subject. This movement is very common in the idiom of Moses, and it merits so much the more attention, because, not having observed it, the greater part of the translators have been mistaken in the meaning of the words and have ridiculously particularized what was universal. As when, for example, in עץ, a vegetable substance, a vegetation in general, they have seen *a wood,* or *a tree:* or in גן, an enclosure, a circumscription, a sphere, only a *garden*: or even in דם, the universal idea of an assimilation of homogeneous parts, they have seen only *blood;* etc.

When a noun is composed of three or more consonants, and when it is of more than one syllable, it is obviously a derivative. It is in the examination of its root that the art of the etymologist shines. He must master both the value of each sign and the position that it takes, whether at the beginning or the end of words, and the different modifications which it brings about; for, to understand the root clearly, it is necessary to know how to distinguish it from the sign, or from the article by which it is modified. If the etymologist would acquire a science which opens the door to the loftiest conceptions, he must be provided with the faculties and the necessary means. If long study of tongues in general, and the Hebraic tongue in particular, can lend a little confidence in my abilities, I beg the reader, interested in an art too little cultivated, to study carefully, both the series of Hebraic roots which I give him at the close of this Grammar and the numerous notes which accompany my translation of the Cosmogony of Moses.

The work of Court de Gébelin is a vast storehouse of words, which one ought to possess without being a slave to it. This painstaking man had intellect rather than etymological genius; he searched well; he classed well his materials; but he constructed badly. His merit, is having introduced the Primitive tongue; his fault, is having introduced it to his reader in a thousand scattered fragments. The genius will consist in reassembling these fragments to form a whole. I offer in this Grammar an instrument to attain this end. It is THE HEBRAIC TONGUE DERIVED WHOLLY FROM THE SIGN.

Here are the general principles which can be drawn from the work of Gébelin relative to etymological science. I add some developments that experience has suggested to me.

Particular tongues are only the dialects of an universal tongue founded upon nature, and of which a spark of the Divine word animates the elements. This tongue, that no people has ever possessed in its entirety, can be called *the Primitive tongue*. This tongue, from which all others spring as from an unique trunk, is composed only of monosyllabic roots, all adhering to a small number of signs. In proportion as the particular tongues become mingled with one another and separated from their primitive stock, the words become more and more altered: therefore it is essential to compare many languages in order to obtain the understanding of a single one.

It is necessary to know that all vowels tend to become consonants, and all consonants to become vowels;

to consider this movement; to follow it in its modifications; to distinguish carefully the mother vowel from the vague vowel and when one is assured that the vocal sound which enters into the composition of a word, descends from a vague vowel, give it no further attention. One will attain to this final understanding, by the study of the Hebraic tongue, where the difference which exists between these two sorts of vowels is decisive.

It is necessary to consider besides, that, in the generation of tongues, the consonants are substituted for one another, particularly those of the same organic sound. Therefore it is well to classify them by the sound and to know them under this new relation.

Labial sound: ב, פ, ו : B, P, PH, F, V. This sound, being the easiest, is the first of which children make use; it is generally that of gentleness and mildness considered as onomatopoetic.

Dental sound: ד, ט : D, T. It expresses, on the contrary, all that which touches, thunders, resounds, resists, protects.

Lingual sound: ל, ר : L, LL, LH, R, RH. It expresses a rapid movement, either rectilinear or circular, in whatever sense one imagines it, always considered as onomatopoetic.

Nasal sound: מ, נ : M, N, GN. It expresses all that which passes from without within, or which emerges from within without.

Guttural sound: ג, כ, ע, ק : GH, ĊH, WH, K, Q. It expresses deep, hollow objects, contained one within the other, or modelled by assimilation.

Hissing sound: ז, ס, צ : Z, S, X, TZ, DZ, PS. It is applied to all hissing objects, to all those which have relation with the air, or which cleave it in their course.

Sibilant sound: י, ש, ת : J, G, CH, SH, TH. It expresses light movements, **soft and durable sounds**; all pleasing objects.

The consonants thus distinguished by sound, become the general signs from which the onomatopoetic roots of which I have spoken, are formed, and are very easily put one in the place of the other. In the derivative tongues they even lend mutual aid in passing from one sound to another, and it is then that they render the etymology of the words more and more uncertain. The etymologist can only surmount the numerous obstacles in the modern idioms, by having stored in his mind a number of tongues whose radical words can assist him readily in going back to the idiomatic or primitive root of the word which he analyzes. Never can one hope by the aid of a single tongue, to form good etymology.

As to the mother vowels, א, ה, ח, ו, ו, י, ע; A, E, Ê, OU, O, I, HO; they are substituted successively one for the other, from א to ע; they all incline to become consonants and to become extinct in the deep and guttural sound כ, which can be represented by the Greek χ or the German *čh*. I always mark this *čh* with an *accent grave* in order to distinguish it from the French *ch*, which is a hissing sound like the ש of the Hebrews, or the *sh* of the English.

After having set forth these etymological principles, I pass on to the next rules, relative to their employment; very nearly such as Court de Gébelin gives them.

One should not take for granted any alteration in a word that one may not be able to prove by usage or by analogy; nor confuse the radical characters of a word with the accessory characters, which are only added signs or articles. The words should be classified by families and none admitted unless it has been grammatically analyzed: primitives, should be distinguished from compounds and all forced etymology carefully avoided: and finally, an historical or moral proof should corroborate the etymology; for the sciences proceed with certain step only as they throw light upon each other.

§ II.

QUALITY

I call Quality, in the Hebraic nouns, the distinction which I establish among them and by means of which I divide them into four classes, namely: substantives, qualificatives, modificatives, and facultatives.

Substantives are applied to all that has physical or moral substance, the existence of which the thought of man admits either by evidence of the senses, or by that of the intellectual faculties. Substantives are proper or common: *proper* when they are applied to a single being, or to a single thing in particular, as מֹשֶׁה *Mosheh* (Moses), נֹחַ *Noah*, מִצְרַיִם *Mitzraim* (Egypt) etc.; *common*, when they are applied to all beings, or to all things of the same kind, as אִישׁ *man* (intelligent being); רֹאשׁ *head* (that which rules or enjoys by its own movement); מֶלֶךְ *king* (a temporal and local deputy); etc.

Qualificatives express the qualities of the substantives and offer them to the imagination under the form which characterizes them. The grammarians in naming them *adjectives,* have given them a denomination too vague to be preserved in a grammar of the nature of this one. This class of nouns expresses more than a simple adjunction; it expresses the very quality or the form of the substance, as in טוֹב *good,* גָּדוֹל *great,* צַדִּיק *just,* עִבְרִי *Hebrew;* etc.

The tongue of Moses is not rich in qualificatives, but it obviates this lack by the energy of its articles, by that of its verbal facultatives and by the various extensions which it gives to its substantives by joining them to certain initial or terminative characters. It has, for example, in the emphatic article הִ, a means of intensity of which it makes great use, either in placing it at the beginning or the end of words. Thus, of נַחַל *a torrent*, it makes נַחְלָה *a very rapid torrent;* of קָפָד *disappearance, absence*, it makes קְפָדָה *an eternal absence, a total disappearance:* מוֹת *death*, it makes הַמוֹתָה *a violent, cruel, sudden death*, etc. Sometimes it adds to this article, the sign of reciprocity ת, to augment its force. Then one finds for עֵזֶר *a support, an aid*, עֶזְרָתָה *a firm support, an accomplished aid;* for אֵימָה *terror*, אֵימָתָה *extreme terror, frightful terror;* for יְשׁוּעָה *safety, refuge*, יְשׁוּעָתָה *an assured safety, an inaccessible refuge;* etc.

The assimilative article כ, forms a kind of qualificative of the noun which it governs. It is thus that one should understand כֵּאלֹהִים *like unto the Gods*, or *divine;* כַּכֹּהֵן *like unto the priest*, or *sacerdotal;* כְעָם *like unto the people*, or *vulgar;* כַּהַיוֹם *like to-day*, or *modern;* etc.

On the other hand, the sign ת placed at the beginning of a word expresses reciprocity. תַּאֲנִיָה *signifies pain, mutual pain.*

The sign מ, when it is initial, is related to exterior action; when final, on the contrary, it becomes expansive and collective. אוֹל signifies *any force whatever*, מָאוֹל *a circumscribed and local force;* אוֹלָם *an exterior, invading force.*

The sign נ, is that of passive action when it is at the head of words; but at the end, it constitutes an augmentative syllable which extends its signification. אֲפָדָה signifies *a veil*, אֲפָדָן *an immense veil, the enclosure of a tent;* גֵוָא *characterizes an extension*, and גֵוָאָן *an unlimited extension, inordinate;* הֵם *expresses a noise*, and הָמוֹן *a frightful noise, a terrible tumult, a revolt;* etc.

I pass over these details of which my footnotes on

the Cosmogony of Moses will afford sufficient examples. It will be enough for me here to indicate the grammatical forms.

The rabbis, in writing modern Hebrew, form the qualificatives by the addition of the character י to the masculine, and the syllable ית, to the feminine. They say, for example, אלהי *divine* (mas.) and אלהית *divine* (fem.). נפשי *spiritual* (mas.) and נפשית *spiritual* (fem.). Then they draw from these qualificatives a mass of substantive nouns, such as אלהות *the divinity;* אולות *fortitude;* נפשות *spirituality;* ידירות *tenderness;* etc. These forms do not belong to primitive Hebrew.

The comparative among qualificatives is not strictly characterized in the Hebraic tongue. When it is established, which is somewhat rare, it is by means of the extractive article מ, or by the preposition מן which corresponds.

The superlative is expressed in many ways. Sometimes one finds either the substantive or the qualificative doubled, in order to give the idea that one has of their force or their extent; sometimes they are followed by an absolute relative to designate that nothing is comparable to them. At other times the adverbial relation מְאֹד *very, very much, as much as possible,* indicates that one conceives them as having attained their measure in good or in evil, according to their nature. Finally one meets different periphrases and different formulas of which I herewith offer several examples.

QUALITY 127

נֹחַ אִישׁ צַדִּיק תָּמִים....	Noah, intelligent being (man), just with integrity (as just as upright).
טוֹב שֵׁם מִשֶּׁמֶן טוֹב:	a good name, of good essence (a name of high repute is the best essence).
טוֹבִים הַשְּׁנַיִם מִן־הָאֶחָד.	good the two of a single one (two are better than one).
רַע רַע: מָטָה מָטָה:	bad, evil (wicked); down, down (beneath).
מִן־הָאָדֹם הָאָדֹם:	among the red, red (much redder).
קָטֹן בַּגּוֹיִם:	small among people (very small).
הָהָר הַטּוֹב הַזֶּה:	a mountain, the good, that one (the best of all).
טוֹב מְאֹד:	good exceedingly (as much as possible).
הַשָּׁמַיִם וּשְׁמֵי הַשָּׁמָיִם:	the heavens and the heaven of heavens.
אֱלֹהֵי אֱלֹהִים וַאֲדֹנֵי הָאֲדֹנִים:	God of Gods and Lord of Lords.
עֶבֶד עֲבָדִים:	servant of the servants.
חֹשֶׁךְ־אֲפֵלָה:	the obscurity of darkness.
שַׁלְהֶבֶתְיָה: מַאְפֶּלְיָה:	the flame of Jah! the darkness of Jah! (extremes).
אַרְזֵי־אֵל:	the cedars of God! (admirable, very beautiful).
עִיר גְּדוֹלָה לֵאלֹהִים:	a great city! according to Him-the-Gods!
אַמִּץ לַאדֹנָי:	strong according to the Lord! (very strong).
בֹּעֲרָה: בִּמְאֹד מְאֹד:	a burning; with might of might.

Modificatives are the substantives or the qualificatives modified either by a simple abstraction of thought, or by the addition of an adverbial relation, so as to become the expression of an action understood. It is not unusual to find in Hebrew, nouns which can be taken, at the same time, as substantives, qualificatives or modificatives; all by a movement of abstraction, and this is easy when the idiom is not far removed from its source. Thus, for example טוֹב *good*, signifies equally *the good*, and the *good* manner in which a thing is done: רַע *evil*, signifies equally that which is *evil*, and the *evil* manner in which a thing is done. One perceives that the words *good* and *evil*, have exactly the same signification as the Hebraic words טוֹב and רַע, as substantives, and that they contain the same qualificative and modificative faculties. I have chosen them expressly so as to show how this abstraction of thought of which I have spoken, is accomplished.

Modificative nouns which are formed by the addition of a designative or adverbial relation as in French, *à-la-mode* (in the fashion), *à-outrance* (to the utmost), *forte-ment* (strongly), *douce-ment* (gently), are very rare in Hebrew. One finds, however, certain ones such as בְּרֵאשִׁית, *in the beginning, in-principle*; יְהוּדִית, *in Jewish*; מֵאֲשׁוּרִית *from the Assyrian;* etc. The nouns of number belong at the same time to substantives, qualificatives and modificatives. אֶחָד, *one*, can signify alike, *unity*, *unique* and *uniquely*.

Facultative nouns are the substantives, *verbalized*, as it were, and in which the absolute verb הוה, *to be-being*, begins to make its influence felt. The grammarians have called them up to this time *participles*, but I treat this weak denomination, as I have treated the one which they have given to qualificatives. I replace it by another which I believe more just.

Facultatives merit particular attention in all tongues, but especially in that of Moses, where they present more openly than in any other, the link which unites the substantive to the verb, and which, by an inexplicable power, makes of a substance inert and without action, an animated substance being carried suddenly toward a determined end. It is by means of the sign of light and of intellectual sense, ו, that this metamorphosis is accomplished. This is remarkable. If I take, for example, the substantive רֶגֶן, which expresses all physical movement all moral affection; if I introduce between the first and second character which compose it, the verbal sign ו, I obtain immediately the *continued* facultative, רוֹגֵן, *to be-moving, affecting, agitating*. If I modify this sign, that is to say, if I give it its convertible nature וֹ, and if I place it between the second and third character of the substantive in question, I obtain then the *finished* facultative רָגוֹן, *to be-moved, affected, agitated*. It is the same with מֶלֶךְ *a king*, whose continued and finished facultatives are מוֹלֵךְ *to be-ruling, governing;* מָלוֹךְ *to be-ruled, governed,* and many others.

It can be observed that I name *continued facultative*, what the grammarians call *present participle*, and *finished* that which they call *past;* because in effect, the action expressed by these facultatives is not, properly speaking, present or past, but continued or finished in any time whatever. One says clearly *it was burning, it is burning, it will be burning; it was burned, it is burned, it will be burned.* Now who cannot see that the facultatives *burning* and *burned,* are by turns, both past, present and future? They both participate in these three tenses with the difference, that the first is always continued and the other always finished.

But let us return. It is from the finished facultative that the verb comes, as I shall demonstrate later on. This facultative, by means of which speech receives verbal life, is formed from the primitive root by the introduction of the sign וֹ, between the two characters of which it is composed. Thus, for example:

The root שׁם contains every idea of elevation, erection, or monument, raised as indication of a place or thing:

thence: שָׁם or שׁוֹם to be erecting, stating, decreeing, designating:

שׁוֹם to be erected, stated, etc., whence the verb שׁוֹם *to erect.*

The root כל contains every idea of consummation, of totalization, of agglomeration, of absorption:

thence: כּוֹל or כָּל to be consummating, totalizing, agglomerating:

כּוֹל to be consummated, agglomerated: whence the verb כּוֹל, *to consummate.*

The root גל expresses every idea of heaping up, lifting up, of movement which carries upward from below:

thence: גּוֹל or גָּל to be heaping up, lifting up, pushing, leaping:

גּוֹל to be heaped up, lifted up; whence the verb גּוֹל, *to heap up.*

As I shall be obliged to return to this formation of the facultatives, in the chapter in which I shall treat of the verb, it is needless for me to dwell further upon it now. I cannot, however, refrain from making the observation that since the institution of the Chaldaic punctuation, the points *kamez, holem,* and even *zere,* have often replaced the verbal sign וֹ in the continued facultative,

QUALITY

whether of compound or radical origin, and that one finds quite commonly רגן *to be moving;* מֶלֶך *to be ruling;* קָם *to be establishing;* מֵת *to be dying;* etc. But two things prove that this is an abuse of punctuation. The first is, that when the continued facultative presents itself in an absolute manner, and when nothing can determine the meaning, then the sign reappears irresistibly; as in the following examples, קוֹם *the action of establishing, or to be establishing:* מוֹת *the action of dying, or to be dying.* The second thing which proves the abuse of which I am speaking, is that the rabbis who preserve to a certain point the oral tradition, never fail to make the mother vowel וֹ, appear in these same facultatives unless they deem it more suitable to substitute its analogues י or אי, writing קוֹם, קים or קאים, *to be establishing, to establish, the action of establishing.*

I shall terminate this paragraph by saying that facultatives both continued and finished, are subject to the same inflections as the substantive and qualificative nouns, that is, of gender, number, movement and construction. The modificative noun does not have the inflections of the others because it contains an implied action, and since it has, as I shall demonstrate, the part of itself which emanates from the verb *to be,* wholly immutable and consequently inflexible.

§ III.

GENDER

Gender is distinguished at first by the sex, male or female, or by a sort of analogy, of similitude, which appears to exist among things, and the sex which is assigned to them by speech. The Hebraic tongue has two genders only, the masculine and the feminine; notwithstanding the efforts that the grammarians have made to discover in it a third and even a fourth which they have called common or epicene. These so-called genders are only the liberty allowed the speaker of giving to such or such substantive the masculine or feminine gender, indifferently, and according to the circumstance: if these genders merit any attention, it is when passing into the derivative tongues, and in taking a particular form there, that they have constituted the neuter gender which one encounters in many of them.

The feminine gender is derived from the masculine, and is formed by adding to the substantive, qualificative or facultative noun, the sign ה which is that of life. The modificative nouns have no gender, because they modify actions and not things, as do the other kinds of words.

I beg the reader who follows me with any degree of interest, to observe the force and constancy with which is demonstrated everywhere, the power that I have attributed to the *sign,* a power upon which I base the whole genius of the tongue of Moses.

I have said that the feminine gender is formed from the masculine by the addition of the sign of life ה: was it possible to imagine a sign of happier expression, to indicate the sex by which all beings appear to owe life, this blessing of the Divinity?

GENDER

Thus מֶלֶךְ *a king,* produces מַלְכָּה *a queen;* חָכָם *a wise man,* חֲכָמָה *a wise woman;* דָּג *a male fish,* דָּגָה *a female fish.*

Thus טוֹב *good* (mas.), becomes טוֹבָה *good* (fem.); גָּדוֹל *great* (mas.), גְּדוֹלָה *great* (fem.).

Thus מוֹלֵךְ *to be ruling* (mas.), becomes מוֹלְכָה *to be ruling* (fem.): שׂוֹם or שָׂם *to be raising* (mas.), שׂוֹמָה *to be raising* (fem.).

It must be observed, in respect to this formation, that when the qualificative masculine is terminated with the character ה, which is then only the emphatic sign, or by the character י, sign of manifestation, these two characters remain wholly simple, or are modified by the sign of reciprocity ת, in the following manner: יָפֶה *beautiful* (mas.), יָפָה or יָפַת (fem.); שֵׁנִי *second* (mas.), שְׁנִיָּה or שֵׁנִית (fem.).

Besides, this sign ת, image of all that is mutual, replaces in almost every case the character ה, when it is a question of the feminine termination of qualificative or facultative nouns; it seems even, that the genius of the Hebraic tongue is particularly partial to it in the latter. One finds נוֹפֶלֶת, rather than נוֹפְלָה, *to be falling;* בּוֹרַחַת, rather than בּוֹרְחָה *to be fleeing;* etc.

It is useless, in a Grammar which treats principally of the genius of a tongue, to expatiate much upon the application of the genders; that is a matter which concerns the dictionary. Let it suffice to know, that, in general, the proper names of men, of occupations, of titles, peoples, rivers, mountains and months, are masculine; whereas the names of women, of countries, of cities, the members of the body, and all substantives terminating with the sign ה, are feminine.

As to the common gender, that is to say, that of the substantive nouns which take the masculine and feminine

134   THE HEBRAIC TONGUE RESTORED

alike, it is impossible to apply any rule even approximately; it is by use alone that it can be shown. These are the substantives of the common gender which come to my mind at the moment: גַן *enclosure, organic sphere;* שֶׁמֶשׁ *sun;* אֶרֶץ *earth;* אוֹת *sign;* עֵת *time;* רוּחַ *spirit, expansive breath;* נֶפֶשׁ *soul;* אָרוֹן *chain of mountains;* חֲזִיר *pig;* אֲרִי *lion;* etc.

§ IV.

NUMBER

There exist only two characteristic numbers in Hebrew; these are *the singular* and *the plural;* the third number, called *dual,* is but a simple restriction of thought, a modification of the plural which tradition alone has been able to preserve by aid of the Chaldaic punctuation. This restricted number, passing into certain derivative tongues, has constituted in them a characteristic number, by means of the forms which it has assumed; but it is obvious that the Hebraic tongue, had it at first either alone, or else distinguished it from the plural only by a simple inflection of the voice, too little evident to be expressed by the sign; for it should be carefully observed that it is never the sign which expresses it, but the punctuation, at least in masculine nouns: as to feminine nouns, which, in the *dual* number, assume the same characters which indicate the masculine plural, one might, strictly speaking, consider them as belonging to common gender.

Masculine nouns, whether substantive, qualificative or facultative, form their plural by the addition of the syllable ים, which, uniting the signs of manifestation and of exterior generation, expresses infinite succession, the immensity of things.

Feminine nouns of the same classes form their plural by the addition of the syllable ות, which, uniting the signs of light and of reciprocity, expresses all that is mutual and similar, and develops the idea of the identity of things.

The two genders of the dual number are formed by the addition of the same syllable ים, designating the masculine plural, to which one adds, according to the Chaldaic punctuation, the vague vowel named *kamez* or *patah*, in this manner: יָם, or יַם. One should realize now that this number is not really characteristic, as I have stated, since, if we remove the Chaldaic punctuation, and if we read the tongue of Moses without points, which should always be done in order to go back to its hieroglyphic source, this number disappears entirely; the dual masculine being absorbed in the plural of the same gender, and the feminine being only an extension of the common number. The modern rabbis who have clearly seen this difficulty (considering the disadvantage of the Chaldaic punctuation, and furthermore, not wishing to loose this third number which presented certain beauties, and had been orally transmitted to them), have adopted the plan of expressing the inflection of the voice which constituted it in its origin, by doubling the sign of manifestation ”, in this manner: רַגְלַיִם *the two feet* יָדַיִם *the two hands*. This number, furthermore, is usually applied to the things which nature has made double, or which the mind conceives as double, as the following examples will demonstrate.

Examples of the masculine plural.

צַדִיק *king,* מְלָכִים *kings;* סֵפֶר *book,* סְפָרִים *books:* מֶלֶךְ *just one,* צַדִיקִים *just ones;* נָקִי *innocent,* נְקִיִים *innocents;* פָקוּד *to be visiting, caring for,* פוֹקְדִים *(plural);* פָקוּד *to be visited, cared for,* פְקוּדִים *(plural);* etc.

Examples of the feminine plural.

מַלְכָה *queen,* מַלְכוֹת *queens;* אֵם *mother,* אִמוֹת *mothers;* פוֹקֶרֶת or פוֹקְדָה *just one,* צְדִיקוֹת *just ones;* צָדִיקָה *to be visiting, caring for,* פוֹקְדוֹת *(plural);* פְקוּדָה *to be visited, cared for,* פְקוּדוֹת *(plural);* etc.

Examples of the dual.

שַׁד *breast,* שָׁדַיִם *both breasts;* יָרֵךְ *thigh,* יְרֵכַיִם *both thighs;* שָׂפָה *lip,* שְׂפָתַיִם *both lips;* מֵי *water:* מַיִם *the waters;* שְׁמֵי *heaven (singular obsolete),* שָׁמַיִם *the heavens;* יָד *hand,* יָדַיִם *both hands;* etc.

It can be observed in these examples that the final character י is sometimes preserved in the plural as in נָקִי *innocent,* נְקִיִּים *innocents;* or in אֲרִי *lion,* אֲרָיִים *lions;* but it is, however, more customary for this final character י, to become lost or amalgamated with the plural, as in יְהוּדִי *a Jew,* יְהוּדִים *the Jews.*

It can also be observed that feminine nouns which terminate in ה in the singular, lose this character in taking the plural, and that those which take the dual number, change this same character to ת, as in שָׂפָה *lip,* שְׂפָתַיִם *both lips;* חוֹמָה *wall,* חמתים *both walls.*

Sometimes the plural number of the masculine in ים, is changed into ין, after the Chaldaic manner, and one finds quite frequently אַחֵר *other,* אַחֲרִין *others;* בֵּן *son,* בְּנִין *sons,* etc.

Sometimes also the feminine plural in וֹת, loses its essential character and preserves only the character ת, preceded thus by the vowel point *holem* as in תּוֹלְדֹת *the symbol of generations* (genealogical tree): צִדְקֹת *righteous acts,* etc. This is also an abuse born of the Chaldaic punctuation, and proves what I have said with regard to the facultatives. The rabbis are so averse to the suppression of this important sign ו in the feminine plural, that they frequently join to it the sign of manifestation י, to give it more force; writing אוֹת *sign, symbol, character,* and אוֹתִיּוֹת *signs, symbols,* etc.

One finds in Hebrew, as in other tongues, nouns which are always used in the singular and others which are always in the plural. Among the former one observes proper names, names of metals, of liquors, of virtues, of vices, etc. Among the latter, the names of ages, and of conditions relative to men.

One finds equally masculine or feminine nouns in the singular which take, in the plural, the feminine or masculine termination inconsistent with their gender; as אָב *father*, אָבוֹת *fathers;* עִיר *city*, עָרִים *cities;* etc. One also finds the gender called common or epicene, which takes indifferently the masculine or feminine plural, as I have already remarked; as הֵיכָל *palace*, הֵיכָלִים or הֵיכָלוֹת *palaces*. But these are anomalies which the grammar of an unspoken tongue can only indicate, leaving to the dictionary the care of noting them in detail.

§ V.

MOVEMENT

I call *Movement,* in the Hebraic nouns, that accidental modification which they undergo by the articles of which I have spoken in the second section of chapter IV.

In the tongues where this Movement takes place by means of the terminations of the nouns themselves, the grammarians have treated it under the denomination of *case;* a denomination applicable to those tongues, but which can only be applied to a tongue so rich in articles as the Hebrew, by an abuse of terms and in accordance with a scholastic routine wholly ridiculous.

I say that the denomination of *case* was applicable to those tongues, the nouns of which experience changes of termination to express their respective modifications; for, as Court de Gébelin has already remarked, these cases are only articles added to nouns, and which have finally amalgamated with them.[1] But the grammarians of the past centuries, always restricted to the Latin or Greek forms, saw only the material in those tongues, and never even suspected that there might have been something beyond. The time has come to seek for another principle in speech and to examine carefully its influence.

As I have dilated sufficiently upon the signification of each article in particular, as well as upon those of the corresponding prepositions, I now pass on without other preamble to the kind of modification which they bring in the nouns and which I call *Movement.*

Now, movement is inflicted in Hebraic nouns according to the number of the articles. We can, therefore, admit seven kinds of movements in the tongue of Moses, including the designative movement which is formed by

[1] Gramm. univers., p. 379.

means of the designative preposition אֶת and without including the enunciative which is expressed without an article.

I shall call this series of movements *Inflection*, and by this term I replace that of declension which should not be used here.

Example of nominal inflection.

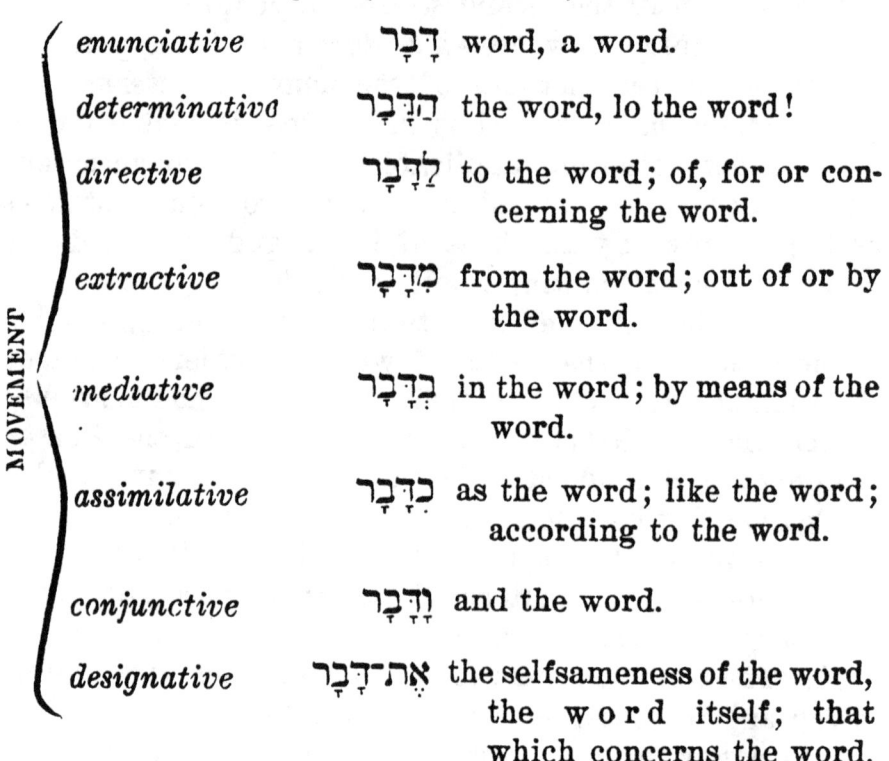

MOVEMENT
{
- *enunciative*   דָּבָר   word, a word.
- *determinative*   הַדָּבָר   the word, lo the word!
- *directive*   לַדָּבָר   to the word; of, for or concerning the word.
- *extractive*   מִדָּבָר   from the word; out of or by the word.
- *mediative*   בַּדָּבָר   in the word; by means of the word.
- *assimilative*   כַּדָּבָר   as the word; like the word; according to the word.
- *conjunctive*   וְדָבָר   and the word.
- *designative*   אֶת־דָּבָר   the selfsameness of the word, the w o r d itself; that which concerns the word.
}

The first remark to make with regard to this nominal inflection is, that the articles which constitute it, being of every gender and every number, are applied to the masculine as to the feminine, to the singular as to the plural or dual.

The second is, that they are often supplied by the corresponding prepositions of which I have spoken, and therefore, that the movement through them acquires greater force; for example, if it is a question of direct movement, the prepositions עַל־, אֱלִי־, אֶל־, which correspond with the article ל, have an energy, drawing nearer, imminent: it is the same with the prepositions מִן, מֵנִי, מִמֶּנִי, which correspond with the extractive article מ: with the prepositions בְּמוֹ, בְּדֵי, בְּ, analogous to the mediative article בּ: the prepositions כְּמוֹ, כָּה, כְּ, which correspond with the assimilative article כּ: all of these augment in the same manner, the force of the movement to which they belong.

The third remark to make is, that the vague vowel which I have indicated by the Chaldaic punctuation, beneath each article, is the one which is found the most commonly used, but not the one which is always encountered. It must be remembered that as this punctuation is only a sort of vocal note applied to the vulgar pronunciation, nothing is more arbitrary than its course. All those Hebraists who are engrossed in the task of determining its variations by fixed rules, are lost in an inextricable labyrinth. I beg the reader who knows how much French or English deviates from the written language by the pronunciation, to consider what a formidable labour it would be, if it were necessary to mark with small accents the sound of each word, often so opposed to the orthography.

Without doubt there are occupations more useful, particularly for the extinct tongues.

The vague vowel, I cannot refrain from repeating, is of no consequence in any way to the meaning of the words of the Hebraic tongue, since one does not wish to speak this tongue. It is to the *sign* that one should give attention: it is its *signification* which must be presented. Considered here as article, it is invariable: it is always ל, ה, מ, ב, כ, or ו, which strikes the eye. What matters it to the ear, whether these characters are followed or not, by a *kamez*, a *patah* or a *zere*, that is to say, the indistinct vowels a, o, e? It is neither the *zere*, nor the *patah* nor the *kamez* which makes them what they are, but their nature as article. The vague vowel is there only for the compass of the voice. Upon seeing it written, it should be pronounced as it is pronounced in the modern tongues without giving it further attention, and if one insists on writing Hebrew from memory, which is, however, quite useless, one should learn to put it down as one learns the orthography, often very arbitrary, of French and English, by dint of copying the words in the manner in which they are written.

The meaning of the article in itself is already sufficiently difficult without still tormenting oneself as to how one shall place a fly speck.

Asiatic idioms in general, and Hebrew in particular, are far from affecting the stiffness of our European idioms. The nearer a word is to its root, the richer it is in pith, so to speak, and the more it can, without ceasing to be itself, develop various significations. The more distant it is, the less it becomes fitting to furnish new ramifications. Also one should guard against believing that an Hebraic word, whatever it may be, can be accurately grasped and rendered in all its acceptations by a modern word. This is not possible. All that can be done is to interpret the acceptation which it presents at the time when it is used. Here, for example, is the word דָּבָר, which I have used in the nominal inflection; I have rendered it by *word;* but in this circumstance where nothing has bound me as to the sense, I might have translated it quite as well by *discourse, precept, commandment, order, sermon, oration;* or by *thing, object, thought, meditation;* or by *term, elocution, expression;* or by the consecrated word *verb*, in Greek λόγος. All these significations and many others that I could add, feel the effects of the root דב, which, formed from the signs of natural abundance, and of active principle, develops the general idea of *effusion;* of the *course* given to anything whatsoever. This root being united by contraction with the root בר, all *creation* of being, offers in the compound דָּבָר, all the means of giving *course* to its ideas, of producing them, of distinguishing them, of creating them exteriorly, to make them known to others.

This diversity of acceptations which must be observed in the words of the Mosaic tongue, must also be observed in the different movements of the nominal inflection. These movements are not, in Hebrew, circumscribed in the limits that I have been obliged to give them. To make them felt in their full extent, it would be necessary to enter into irksome details. I shall give a few examples.

Let us remark first that the article ה, is placed, not only at the head of words as determinative, or at the end as emphatic, but that it becomes also redundant by resting at either place, whereas the other articles act. Thus, one finds הַשָׁמַיִם, *the heavens*, שָׁמַיְמָה *heavens*, הַשָׁמַיְמָה *o heavens!* לְהַשָׁמַיִם *to the heavens, toward the heavens,* אֶת־הַשָׁמַיְמָה *the heavens themselves, that which constitutes the heavens.*

Such are the most common acceptations of this article: but the Hebraic genius by the extension which it gives them, finds the means of adding still a local, intensive, generative, vocative, interrogative and even relative force. Here are some examples.

Locative Force.

הָעִיר: הַפְּלִשְׁתִּים: in the city; toward Palestine.

הָאֹהֱלָה שָׂרָה אִמּוֹ: in the tent of Sarah his mother.

אַרְצָה: שָׁמַיְמָה: on earth; in heaven.

צָפוֹנָה וָנֶגְבָּה וְקֵדְמָה וָיָמָּה: toward the north and toward the south, and the east and the west.

Intensive Force.

נַחֲלָה: עֲפָתָה: a rapid torrent: a profound obscurity.

אֵימָתָה ׃ הַמּוֹתָה ׃ an extreme terror; a violent death.

Generative Force.

אֶת־הָאָרֶץ ׃ selfsameness of the earth: that which constitutes it.
הַמִּזְבַּח הַנְחֹשֶׁת ׃ the altars of brass.
הַמַּמְלְכוֹת הָאָרֶץ ׃ the kingdoms of the earth.
הַמִּסְגְּרוֹת הַגּוֹיִם ׃ the abomination of the peoples.

Vocative Force.

הַיָּם הֶהָרִים ׃ o waters! o mountains!
הַבַּת יְרוּשָׁלַיִם ׃ o daughters of Jerusalem!
בֹּאִי הָרוּחַ ׃ הַיֹּשְׁבִי ׃ come, o spirit, o thou who dwellest!

Interrogative Force.

הַכְּתֹנֶת בִּנְךָ הוּא ׃ is that the tunic of thy son?
הַיֵּיטַב ׃ הַרְאִיתֶם ׃ was it good? did you see?
הַאֱמֶת ׃ הַעֵת ׃ הַאָנֹכִי ׃ is it the truth? is it the time? is it I?

Relative Force.

בֶּן־הַנֵּכָר הַנִּלְוָה ׃ the son of the stranger who was come.
הַנּוֹלַד־לוֹ ׃ he who was born to him.
הָרֹפֵא ׃ הַגּוֹאֵל ׃ he who is healing; he who is redeeming.

The other articles without having so extended a use, have nevertheless their various acceptations. I give here a few examples of each of the movements which they express.

MOVEMENT

Directive Movement.

מִזְמוֹר לְדָוִד׃	the canticle of David.
לְמֶלֶךְ׃ לְהָעָם׃ לְהַמִּזְבֵּחַ׃	for the king: for the people: for the altar.
לָנֶצַח׃ לְעַד׃ לְשֹׂבַע׃	forever: for eternity: to satiety.
אֶל־הַשָּׁמַיִם׃ עַל־הָאָרֶץ׃	toward the heavens: upon the earth.
לְמִינֵהוּ׃	according to his kind.

Extractive Movement.

מֵרֹב׃ מִכֹּהֵן׃	among the multitude: among the priesthood.
מֵיהוָה׃ מִלְאֹם׃	by Yahweh: by the nation.
מִגְּבוּרָתָם׃ מִלִּבּוֹ׃	by means of their power: from the depths of his heart.
מֵעָצְבֵּךְ וּמֵרָגְזֵךְ׃	with thy pain and thine emotion.
לְמִבָּרִאשׁוֹנָה׃	as it was from the beginning.
מִן־הָאָרֶץ׃	beyond the land.
מִימֵי רָע׃ מִקְצֵה הָאָרֶץ׃	from the days of evil: from the end of the earth.

Mediative Movement.

בְּשֵׁבֶט בַּרְזֶל׃	by means of a rod of iron.
בִּנְעָרֵינוּ וּבִזְקֵנֵנוּ׃	with our young men and with our old men.
בֶּחֳדָשִׁים׃	in the festivals of the new moon.
בְּהַשָּׁמַיִם׃ בְּהַדֶּרֶךְ׃	to the heavens: on the way.

Assimilative Movement.

כְּעָם ׃ כַּכֹּהֵן ׃ כְּעֶבֶד ׃	like the p e o p l e: like the priest: like the servant.
כְּהֶחָכָם ׃ כְּהַיּוֹם ׃	like the wise man: the same as to-day.
כְּהַחַלּוֹנוֹת ׃ כְּאַלְפַּיִם ׃	like the windows: about two thousand.
כְּגֵר כָּאֶזְרָח ׃	stranger as well as native.

Conjunctive Movement.

חָכְמָה וְדַעַת ׃	wisdom and knowledge.
וְרֶכֶב וְסוּס ׃	the chariot and the horse.
עַם גָּדוֹל וְרַב וָרָם ׃	the great nation both numerous and powerful.

Designative Movement.

אֶת־הַשָּׁמַיִם וְאֶת־הָאָרֶץ ׃	the sameness of the heavens and the sameness of the earth.
אֶת־הַדָּבָר הַזֶּה ׃	the e s s e n c e of that same thing.
אֶת־נֹחַ ׃	with Noah.
אֶת־שֵׁם וְאֶת־חָם וְאֶת־יָפֶת ׃	Shem himself, and Ham himself, and Japheth himself.

These examples few in number, are sufficient to awaken the attention; but understanding can only be obtained by study.

§ VI.

CONSTRUCT STATE

Hebraic nouns, being classed in the rhetorical sentence according to the rank which they should occupy in developing the thought in its entirety, undergo quite commonly a slight alteration in the final character; now this is what I designate by the name of *construct state*.

In several of the derivative tongues, such as Greek and Latin, this accidental alteration is seen in the termination of the governed noun; it is quite the opposite in Hebrew. The governed noun remains nearly always unchanged, whereas the governing noun experiences quite commonly the terminative alteration of which we are speaking. I call the noun thus modified *construct*, because it determines the construction.

Here in a few words are the elements of this modification.

Masculine or feminine nouns in the singular, terminated by a character other than ה, undergo no other alteration in becoming constructs; when the Hebraic genius wishes, however, to make the construct state felt, it connects them with the noun which follows with a hyphen.

   פֶּתַח־הָאֹהֶל׃ the door of the tent.

   תָּם־לְבָבִי׃ the integrity of my heart.

This hyphen very frequently takes the place of the construct, even when the latter itself could be used.

   סְאָה־סֹלֶת׃ a measure of meal.

   עֲלֵה־זַיִת׃ a branch of the olive tree.

One recognizes, nevertheless, three masculine substantives which form their construct singular, by the addition of the character יֹ: these are אָב *father*, אָח *brother*, and חָם *father-in-law;* one finds:

אֲבִי כְנָעַן : the father of Canaan.

אֲחִי יֶפֶת : חָמִיהָ : the brother of Japheth; father-in-law of her.

But these three substantives are rarely constructed in this manner except with proper nouns, or with the nominal relations called *affixes*, of which I shall speak in the chapter following.

Feminine nouns terminating in ה, and masculine nouns which have received this final character as emphatic article, change it generally into ת.

יְפַת מַרְאֶה : beautiful of form.

עֲשֶׂרֶת הַדְּבָרִים : the ten commandments.

עֲצַת גּוֹיִם : the counsel of the peoples.

Masculine nouns in the plural lose the final character ם, in becoming constructs; feminine nouns add to their plural the character יֹ, and lose in the dual the character ם, as do the masculine. But feminine constructs in the plural are only used with *affixes*. Masculine constructs, in the plural and in the dual, like feminine constructs in the dual, are, on the contrary, constantly employed in the oratorical phrase, as can be judged by the following examples.

תּוֹרֵי זָהָב : the ornaments of gold.

מֵי הַמַּבּוּל : דְּגֵי הַיָּם : the waters of the deluge: the fish of the sea.

כְּלֵי בֵית־יְהוָֹה : the vessels of the house of Yahweh.

יְמֵי שְׁנֵי־חַיֵּי אַבְרָהָם : the days (or luminous periods) of the years (or temporal mutations) of the lives of Abraham.

It is easy to see in these examples that all the plurals terminating in ים, as שָׁנִים, יָמִים, כֵּלִים, דָּגִים, מַיִם, תּוֹרִים, חַיִּים, have lost their final character in the construct state.

I refrain from enlarging my Grammar on this subject, for I shall have occasion to refer again to the construct state in speaking of the affixes which join themselves only to nominal and verbal constructs.

§ VII.

SIGNIFICATION

The Signification of nouns results wholly from the principles which I have laid down. If these principles have been developed with enough clarity and simplicity for an observant reader to grasp the *ensemble,* the signification of nouns should be no longer an inexplicable mystery whose origin he can, like Hobbes or his adherents, attribute only to chance. He must feel that this *signification,* so called from the primordial *signs* where it is in germ, begins to appear under a vague form and is developed under general ideas in the roots composed of these signs; that it is restrained or is fixed by aid of the secondary and successive signs which apply to these roots; finally, that it acquires its whole force by the transformation of these same roots into nouns, and by the kind of movement which the signs again impart to them, appearing for the third time under the denomination of articles.

CHAPTER VI.

NOMINAL RELATIONS.

§ I.

Absolute Pronouns.

I have designated the nominal relations under the name of *pronouns,* so as not to create needlessly new terms.

I divide the pronouns of the Hebraic tongue into two classes; each subdivided into two kinds. The first class is that of the *absolute pronouns,* or pronouns, properly so-called; the second is that of the *affixes,* which are derivatives, whose use I shall explain later.

The pronouns, properly so-called, are relative to persons or things; those relative to persons are called *personal;* those relative to things are named simply *relative.*

The affixes indicate the action of persons or things themselves upon things, and then I name them *nominal affixes;* or they can express the action of the verb upon persons or things and then I give them the name of *verbal affixes.* Below, is the list of the personal and relative pronouns.

Personal Pronouns.

	Singular			Plural	
1 {mas. / fem.}	אָנֹכִי or אֲנִי	I	1 {mas. / fem.}	אֲנַחְנוּ or נַחְנוּ	we
2 {mas. / fem.}	אַתָּה / אַתְּ	thou	2 {mas. / fem.}	אַתֶּם / אַתֵּן	ye
3 {mas. / fem.}	הוּא / הוּא or הִיא	he / she	3 {mas. / fem.}	הֵם / הֵן	they

Relative Pronouns.

Of every Gender and of every Number.

אֵל or אֵלֶה this, that, these; those.

אֲשֶׁר who, which, whom, whose, that which; what.

דָּא, דִּי or דַּן this, that, these, those. (*Chaldaic.*)

זֶה, זוּ or זֹאת this, that, these, those.

הָא this, that, these, those; lo! behold!

הִנֵּה, הֵן lo! behold! is there?

הֲל is it? (interrogation sign).

מִי who? מָה what?

פֹּה that thing there, that place there. (*Egyptian.*)

I have a few remarks to make concerning this class of pronouns. The first is, that I present the table according to the modern usage, which gives the first rank to the pronoun *I* or *me;* and that in this, I differ from the ideas of the rabbis, who, after a false etymology given to the verb, have judged that the rank belonged to the pronoun *he* or *him*. It is not that I am unaware of the mystical reasons which lead certain of them to think that the preëminence belongs to the pronoun of the third person הוּא, *he* or *him,* as forming the basis of the Sacred Name given to the Divinity. What I have said in my notes explaining the Hebraic names אֱלֹהִים and יְהֹוָה proves it adequately; but these reasons, very strong as they appear to them, have not determined me in the least to take away from the personal pronoun אֲנִי or אָנֹכִי *I* or *me,* a rank which belongs to its nature. It is sufficient, in order to feel this rank, to put it into the mouth of the Divinity Itself, as Moses has frequently done: אָנֹכִי יְהֹוָה אֱלֹהֶיךָ, *I am* YAHWEH (*the Being-Eternal*), ÆLOHIM (HE-*the-Gods*) *thine.* It is also sufficient to remember that one finds אֶהְוָה written in the first person, and that therefore, this name has a greater force than YAHWEH.

The second remark that I have to make is, that all these pronouns, personal as well as relative when they are used in an absolute manner, always involve the idea of the verb *to be*, in its three tenses, following the meaning of the phrase, and without the need of expressing it, as in the greater part of the modern idioms. Thus אֲנִי, אַתָּה, הוּא, etc., signifies literally: *I-being*, or *I am, I was, I shall be: thou-being*, or *thou art, thou wast, thou shalt be: he-being*, or *he is, he was, he shall be;* etc. It is the same with all the others indiscriminately.

The third remark finally, concerns the etymology of these pronouns: an etymology worthy of great attention, as it is derived from my principles and confirms them.

Let us content ourselves with examining the first three persons אֲנִי, אַתָּה and הוּא, so as not to increase the examples too much, besides leaving something for the reader to do, who is eager to learn.

Now, what is the root of the first of these pronouns? It is אן, where the united signs of power and of produced being, indicate sufficiently a sphere of activity, an individual existence, acting from the centre to the circumference. This root, modified by the sign of potential manifestation י, which we shall presently see become the affix of possession, designates the *I*, active, manifested and possessed.

The root of the second pronoun אַתָּה, is not less expressive. One sees here as in the first, the sign of power א, but which, united now to that of the reciprocity of things ת, characterizes a mutual power, a coexistent being. One associates with this idea, that of veneration, in joining to the root את, the emphatic and determinative article ה.

But neither the pronoun of the first person, nor that of the second, is equal in energy to that of the third הוּא particularly when it is used in an absolute manner: I must acknowledge it, notwithstanding what I have said concerning the grammatical rank that ought to be accorded the pronoun אֲנִי. This energy is such that uttered in an universal sense, it has become throughout the Orient, one of the sacred names of the Divinity. The Arabs and all the peoples who profess Islamism, pronounce it even in this day, with the greatest respect. One can still remember the righteous indignation of the Turkish ambassador, when this sacred name was profaned in our theatre in the farce of *le Bourgeois-Gentilhomme,* and travestied in the ridiculous syllable *hou! hou!*

Here is its composition. The sign of power א, which as we have seen, appears in the first two pronouns, אֲנִי and אַתָּה, forms also the basis of this one. As long as this sign is governed only by the determinative article ה, it is limited to presenting the idea of a determined being, as is proved by the relative הא: even though the convertible sign ו, adds to it a verbal action, it is still only the pronoun of the third person; a person, considered as acting beyond us, without reciprocity, and that we designate by a root which depicts splendour and elevation, *he* or *him:* but when the character ה, instead of being taken as a simple article, is considered in its state of the sign of universal life, then this same pronoun הוא, leaving its determination, becomes the image of the All-Powerful: that which can be attributed only to GOD!

§ II.

Affixes.

Those of the affixes which I have called *nominal*, are joined without intermediary to the construct noun, to express dependence and possession in the three pronominal persons; for the Hebraic tongue knows not the use of the pronouns called by our grammarians, *possessive*.

Verbal affixes are those which are joined without intermediaries to verbs, whatever their modifications may be, and express the actual action either upon persons or upon things: for neither do the Hebrews know the pronouns that our grammarians call *conjunctive*.

Without further delay, I now give a list of the nominal and verbal affixes.

Nominal.

Singular

1	m. / f.	י or נִי	my, mine
2	m.	ךָ or כה	thy, thine
	f.	ךְ or כִי	
3	m.	וּ, וֹ, הוּ	his, his
	f.	הָ or נָה	her, hers

Plural

1	m. / f.	נוּ	our, ours
2	m.	כֶם	your, yours
	f.	כֶן	
3	m.	ם ,הֶם or מוֹ	their, theirs
	f.	הֶן ,ן	

Verbal.

Singular

$$1 \begin{Bmatrix} m. \\ f. \end{Bmatrix} \text{ נִי or יִ } \text{ of me}$$

$$2 \begin{Bmatrix} m. & \text{כָה or ךָ} \\ f. & \text{כִי or ךְ} \end{Bmatrix} \text{ of thee}$$

$$3 \begin{Bmatrix} m. & \text{הוּ, וּ, or וֹ } \text{ of him} \\ f. & \text{נָה or הָ } \text{ of her} \end{Bmatrix}$$

Plural

$$1 \begin{Bmatrix} m. \\ f. \end{Bmatrix} \text{ נוּ } \text{ of us}$$

$$2 \begin{Bmatrix} m. & \text{כֶם} \\ f. & \text{כֶן} \end{Bmatrix} \text{ of you}$$

$$3 \begin{Bmatrix} m. & \text{מוֹ or ם, כה} \\ f. & \text{הֶן or ן} \end{Bmatrix} \text{ of them}$$

It can be seen, in comparing these two lists, that the nominal and verbal affixes in the Hebraic tongue differ not in the least as to form, but only as to sense. However I must mention that one finds the simplest of these pronouns such as יִ, ךְ, וֹ, etc., used quite generally as nominal affixes, and the most composite such as נִי, כָה, הוּ as verbal affixes, but it is not an invariable rule.

When the personal pronouns אֲנִי *I*, אַתָּה *thou*, הוּא *he*, etc., are subject to the inflection of the articles, it is the nominal affixes which are used in determining the different movements as is shown in the following example:

AFFIXES 157

Example of the Pronominal Inflection.

Singular

Enunciative	אֲנִי	I
Determinative	הָאנֹכִי	it is I!
Directive	לִי	to me
Extractive	מִנִּי ׃ מִמֶּנִּי	from me
Mediative	בִּי ׃ כְּדִי	in me, with me
Assimilative	כִּי ׃ כָּמוֹנִי	as I
Conjunctive	וְאֲנִי	and I
Designative	אוֹתִי ׃ אוֹתֵנִי	myself, me

(all braced as MOVEMENT)

Plural

נַחְנוּ	we
הָאֲנַחְנוּ	us! it is us!
לָנוּ	to us
מֶנּוּ ׃ מִמֶּנּוּ	from us
בָּנוּ	in us, with us
כָּנוּ ׃ כָּמוֹנוּ	as we
וְנַחְנוּ	and we
אוֹתֵנוּ	ourselves

I have chosen, in giving this example, the pronoun of the first person, which will suffice to give an idea of all the others. It will be noticed that I have added to the preposition את of the designative movement, the sign וֹ, because the Hebraic genius affects it in this case and in some others, as giving more importance to this movement.

The designative relations which I have made known under the name of prepositions, are joined to the nominal affixes in the same manner as the articles. Here are some examples of this liaison.

אֵלַי : אֵלֶיךָ : אֲלֵיהֶם :	unto me, unto thee, unto them.
אֶצְלוֹ : אִתּוֹ :	beside him; with him.
בַּעֲדוֹ : בַּעֲדֵיהֶם :	for him; for them.
עָלַי : תַּחְתַּי : עָדַי :	upon me; under me; as far as me.
עִמִּי : עִמְּךָ : עִמּוֹ :	with me; with thee; with him.

Relative pronouns are inflected with articles and with prepositions in the same manner as nouns. I shall not stop to give any particular examples of this inflection which has nothing very remarkable. I prefer to illustrate it by the following phrases:

אֵלֶה תוֹלְדוֹת :	these are the symbols of the generations.
אֲשֶׁר עָשָׂה :	that which he had done.
אָנֹכִי יְהוָֹה אֱלֹהֶיךָ אֲשֶׁר....	I am YAHWEH, HE-THE-GODS thine, who....
וְכָל אֲשֶׁר.....	and all that which...
מַה־זֹּאת עָשִׂיתָ :	why hast thou done that?
מִי־אַתְּ : מִי־אֵלֶּה :	who art thou? who are those?
מִי־שְׁמֶךָ : מַה קוֹל :	what is thy name? what is this voice?
מַה מִּשְׁפַּט הָאִישׁ :	what is the fashion of this man?
מַה־טּוֹב וּמַה־נָּעִים :	how good it is! how pleasing!
מֶה־הָיָה לוֹ :	what has happened to him?
בַּת־מִי אַתְּ :	the daughter of whom art thou?

AFFIXES

לְמִי הַנַּעֲרָה הַזֹּאת׃	to whom belongs the young woman there?
לָמָה לִּי׃ עַל־מָה׃	why mine? upon what?
עַל־מָה שָׁוְא׃	upon what futility?
הִנְנִי׃ הִנֶּנּוּ׃ כֻּלָּנוּ׃ כֻּלְּכֶם׃	here am I: behold us: both: them all.
כָּזֶה׃ כָּהֵנָּה׃	like this one; like that one.
כָּזֶה וְכָזֶה׃	like this and like that.
בָּזֶה׃ כָּאֵלֶּה׃	in this one: in that one.

The relative אֲשֶׁר whose use I have just shown in several examples, has this peculiarity, that it furnishes a sort of pronominal article which is quite commonly employed.

This article, the only one of its kind, is reduced to the character שׁ, and comprises in this state all the properties of the sign which it represents. Placed at the head of nouns or verbs, it implies all the force of relative movement. Sometimes in uniting itself to the directive article לְ, it forms the pronominal preposition שֶׁל, which then participates in the two ideas of relation and direction contained in the two signs of which it is composed.

It is most important in studying Hebrew, to have the foregoing articles ever present in the mind, as well as those which I give below; for the Hebraists, unceasingly confusing them with the nouns that they inflect, have singularly corrupted the meaning of several passages. Here are a few examples which can facilitate understanding the prenominal articles in question.

עַד שַׁקַּמְתִּי׃	as much as I was opposed, so much was I strengthened.
שֶׁהָיָה לָנוּ׃ שֶׁלִּי׃	who was for us? who, for me?
שֶׁאַתָּה׃ שֶׁהוּא׃ שֶׁיְהֹוָה׃	for whom thou: for whom he: for whom YAHWEH.

שִׁכָבָה : בְּשֶׁגָּם :	whose fellow-creature? in what also?
שַׁלָּמָה :	what therefore? What is the why (the cause).
שֶׁאָהֲבָה .... שֵׁיֵרֵד	that which she loved... That which descends...
שֶׁעָבַרְתִּי	that which I passed over...
כְּנַף־הַמְּעִיל־שֶׁל־שָׁאוּל :	the border of the tunic which was Saul's.
מִשֶּׁלָּנוּ :	of that which is ours.
בְּשֶׁלְּמִי הָרָעָה :	in that which is the why (the cause) of evil.

§ III.

Use of the Affixes.

Let us examine now, the use of nominal affixes with nouns: later on we shall examine that of verbal affixes with verbs. These affixes are placed, as I have already stated, without intermediary after the nouns, to express dependence or possession in the three pronominal persons. It is essential to recall here what I said in speaking of the construct state; for it is the affix which makes a construct of every noun.

Thus, among the masculine nouns which do not terminate with ה, three only take the character י, in the construct singular, that is: אבי *father,* אחי *brother,* and חמי *father-in-law,* the others remain inflexible.

Thus, among the masculine and feminine nouns, all those which terminate in ה, or which have received this character as an emphatic article, change this character in the singular, to ת.

Thus, all of the masculine nouns terminating in the plural with י׳, lose the character ם in becoming constructs; it is the same with the dual for both genders.

Thus, generally, but in a manner less irresistible, the feminine whose plural is formed with וֹת, adds י to this final syllable in taking the nominal affix.

This understood, I pass now to the examples.

Mas. Sing. { enunciative / construct } דָּבָר the word

SING. PERS.
1 { mas. / fem. } דְּבָרִי my word
2 { mas. דְּבָרְךָ / fem. דְּבָרֵךְ } thy word
3 { mas. דְּבָרוֹ his / fem. דְּבָרָהּ her } word

PLU. PERS.
1 { mas. / fem. } דְּבָרֵנוּ our word
2 { mas. דְּבַרְכֶם / fem. דְּבַרְכֶן } your word
3 { mas. דְּבָרָם / fem. דְּבָרָן } their word

Mas. Plu. { enunciative דְּבָרִים / construct דִּבְרֵי } the words

SING. PERS.
1 { mas. / fem. } דְּבָרַי my words
2 { mas. דְּבָרֶיךָ / fem. דְּבָרַיִךְ } thy words
3 { mas. דְּבָרָיו his / fem. דְּבָרֶיהָ her } words

USE OF AFFIXES

PLU. PERS.
- 1 {mas. / fem.} דְּבָרֵינוּ — our words
- 2 {mas. דְּבָרֵיכֶם / fem. דְּבָרֵיכֶן} your words
- 3 {mas. דִּבְרֵיהֶם / fem. דִּבְרֵיהֶן} their words

Fem. Sing. { enunciative צָרָה / construct צָרַת } the distress

SING. PERS.
- 1 {mas. / fem.} צָרָתִי — my distress
- 2 {mas. צָרָתְךָ / fem. צָרָתֵךְ} thy distress
- 3 {mas. צָרָתוֹ his / fem. צָרָתָהּ her} distress

PLU. PERS.
- 1 {mas. / fem.} צָרָתֵנוּ — our distress
- 2 {mas. צָרַתְכֶם / fem. צָרַתְכֶן} your distress
- 3 {mas. צָרָתָם / fem. צָרָתָן} their distress

Fem. Plu. { *enunciative* צָרוֹת
construct צָרוֹתֵי } the distresses

SING. PERS.
1 { *mas.* / *fem.* } צָרוֹתַי my distresses
2 { *mas.* צָרוֹתֶיךָ / *fem.* צָרוֹתַיִךְ } thy distresses
3 { *mas.* צָרוֹתָיו his, / *fem.* צָרוֹתֶיהָ her } distresses

PLU. PERS.
1 { *mas.* / *fem.* } צָרוֹתֵינוּ our distresses
2 { *mas.* צָרוֹתֵיכֶם / *fem.* צָרוֹתֵיכֶן } your distresses
3 { *mas.* צָרוֹתֵיהֶם / *fem.* צָרוֹתֵיהֶן } their distresses

Mas. or fem. dual { *enunciative* עֵינַיִם
construct עֵינֵי } the eyes

SING. PERS.
1 { *mas.* / *fem.* } עֵינַי my eyes
2 { *mas.* עֵינֶיךָ / *fem.* עֵינַיִךְ } thine eyes
3 { *mas.* עֵינָיו his / *fem.* עֵינֶיהָ her } eyes

USE OF AFFIXES

PLU. PERS.
- 1 { mas. / fem. } עֵינֵינוּ *our eyes*
- 2 { mas. עֵינֵיכֶם / fem. עֵינֵיכֶן } *your eyes*
- 3 { mas. עֵינֵיהֶם / fem. עֵינֵיהֶן } *their eyes*

Nouns, whether masculine or feminine, which take the common or dual number, follow in the singular, one of the preceding examples according to their gender.

The anomalies relative to the vague vowel marked by the Chaldaic punctuation are still considerable: but they have no effect, and should not delay us. The only important remark to make is, that often the affix of the third person masculine of the singular, is found to be הוּ or מוֹ in place of וֹ and again in the plural מוֹ in place of ם, or of הם: so that one might find דְּבָרֵהוּ or דְּבָרְמוֹ *his word*, and דְּבָרֵימוֹ *his words* or *their words;* or צָרָתֵהוּ or צָרָתֵמוֹ *his distress*, and צָרוֹתֵימוֹ *his distresses* or *their distresses*. Besides it seems that the affix הוּ, may be applied to the emphatic style, and the affix מוֹ, to poetry.

CHAPTER VII.

THE VERB

§ I.

Absolute Verb and Particular Verbs.

If in the course of this Grammar I have been compelled, in order to be understood, to speak often of the plural verbs, it must not be thought for this reason, that I have forgotten my fundamental principle, namely, that there exists but one sole Verb: a principle which I believe fixed. The plural verbs, of which I have spoken, should only be understood as nouns *verbalized* as it were, by the unique Verb הוה *to be-being,* in which it develops its influence with more or less force and intensity. Let us forget therefore, the false ideas which we have kept through habit, of a mass of verbs existing by themselves, and return to our principle.

There is but one Verb.

The words to which one has ordinarily given the name of verbs, are only substantives animated by this single verb, and determined toward the end peculiar to them: for now we can see that the verb, in communicating to nouns the verbal life which they possess, changes in no respect their inner nature, but only makes them living with the life whose principles they held concealed within themselves. Thus the flame, communicated to all combustible substance, burns not only as flame but as enflamed substance, good or evil, according to its intrinsic quality.

The unique Verb of which I speak is formed in Hebrew, in a manner meriting the attention of the reader. Its principle is light, represented by the intellectual sign ו; its substance is life universal and absolute, represented by the root הו. This root, as I have before stated, never leaves the noun: for when it is a question of designating life proper, or, to express it better, *existence*,—which men ought never to confuse with *life,* the Hebraic tongue employs the root חי, in which the character ח, carries the idea of some sort of effort causing equilibrium between two opposed powers. It is by means of intellectual light, characterized by the sign ו, that this unique Verb dispenses its verbal force to nouns, and transforms them into particular verbs.

The verb in itself is immutable. It knows neither number nor gender; it has no kind of inflection. It is foreign to forms, to movement and to time, as long as it does not leave its absolute essence and as long as the thought conceives it independent of all substance. הוה *to be-being,* belongs to the masculine as well as to the feminine, to the singular as to the plural, to active movement as to passive movement; it exercises the same influence upon the past as upon the future; it fulfills the present; it is the image of a duration without beginning and without end: הוה *to be-being* fulfills all, comprehends all, animates all.

But in this state of absolute immutability and of universality, it is incomprehensible for man. When it acts independently of substance man cannot grasp it. It is only because of the substance which it assumes, that it is sentient. In this new state it loses its immutability. The substance which it assumes transmits to it nearly all its forms; but these same forms that it influences, acquire particular modifications through which an experienced eye can still distinguish its inflexible unity.

These details may appear extraordinary to the grammarians but little accustomed to find these sorts of speculations in their works; but I have forewarned them that it is upon the Hebraic grammar that I am writing and not upon any from their domain. If they consider my method applicable, as I think it is, they may adopt it; if they do not, nothing hinders them from following their own routine.

Let us continue. As the verb הוה becomes manifest only because of the substance which it has assumed, it participates in its forms. Therefore, every time that it appears in speech, it is with the attributes of a particular verb, and subject to the same modifications. Now, these modifications in particular verbs, or rather in facultative nouns verbalized, are four in number, namely, Form, Movement, Time and Person.

I shall explain later what these modifications are and in what manner they act upon the verbs; it is essential to examine first of all, how these verbs issue from the primitive roots or derivative nouns, subject to the unique Verb which animates them.

If we consider the unique Verb הוה, *to be-being,* as a particular verb, we shall see clearly that what constitutes it as such, is the intellectual sign ו, in which the verbal *esprit* appears wholly to reside. The root הה, by itself, is only a vague exclamation, a sort of expiration, which, when it signifies something, as in the Chinese tongue, for example, is limited to depicting the breath, its exhalation, its warmth, and sometimes the life that this warmth infers; but then the vocal sound *o* is soon manifest, as can be seen in *ho, houo, hoe,* Chinese roots, which express all ideas of warmth, of fire, of life, of action and of being.

The sign ו, being constituted, according to the genius of the Hebraic tongue, symbol of the universal verb, it is evident that in transferring it into a root or into any compound whatsoever of this tongue, this root or this compound will partake instantly of the verbal nature: for this invariably happens.

We have seen in treating particularly of the sign, that the one in question is presented under two distinct modifications, first, as the universal convertible sign ו, and second, as the luminous sign וֹ: these two modifications are employed equally in the formation of verbs. I have already spoken of this in dealing with the facultatives in the Second section of the Fifth chapter. Here it is only a matter of verbs.

The facultative by which the Hebraic genius brings out the verbal action, is the finished facultative. It is in this manner.

This facultative is formed from roots by the insertion of the sign ו, between the two characters which compose it, as שׂוּם to be placed, גּוּל to be exhausted; and from compound nouns by the insertion of this same sign between the last two characters of these nouns, as רגוּן to be moved, מָלוּךְ to be ruled.

Now if we take the finished facultative coming from the root, it will be sufficient, by a simple abstraction of thought, to make a verb of it, in that sort of original state which the grammarians call *infinitive*, though I cannot very well see why, and which I call, *nominal*, because it is governed by the articles and is subject to the nominal inflection. And as to the finished facultative coming from the compounds, we make a nominal verb of it by enlightening the sign ו that is to say, replacing it with the sign וֹ, as the following example illustrates:

root קם: every idea of substance and of material establishment

finished facultative קוּם: to be established

nominal verb קוֹם: the action of establishing

compound רֶגֶן: physical or moral movement; an emotion

finished facultative רְגֻן: to be moved

nominal verb רְגוֹן: the action of moving

ABSOLUTE VERB AND PARTICULAR VERBS 171

It is well to observe that sometimes ו is enlightened in order to form the verb from the root, as in מוט *to waver,* and in some others. As to the nominal verbs coming from compounds, the rule is without exception in this respect. If the Chaldaic punctuation replaces this sign by the points *holem* or *kamez* these points have then the same value and that suffices. This abuse due to the indolence of the copyists was inevitable.

§ II.

Three kinds of Particular Verbs.

There is no need I think of calling attention to the effect of the convertible sign, which, insinuating itself into the heart of the primitive roots, makes them pass from the state of noun to that of verb, and which being enlightened or extinguished by turn, and changing its position in the compound substantives, produces the sentiment of an action, continued or finished, and as it were, fixes the verbal life by the successive formation of the two facultatives and the nominal verb. I believe that there is none of my readers who, having reached this point of my Grammar, and being impressed by this admirable development does not disdainfully reject any system tending to make of speech a mechanical art or an arbitrary institution.

Indeed! if speech were a mechanical art or an arbitrary institution as has been advanced by Hobbes, and before him by Gorgias and the sophists of his school, could it, I ask, have these profound roots which, being derived from a small quantity of signs and being blended not only with the very elements of nature, but also producing those immense ramifications which, coloured with all the fires of genius, take possession of the domain of thought and seem to reach to the limits of infinity? Does one see anything similar in games of chance? Do human institutions, however perfect they may be, ever have this progressive course of aggrandizement and force? Where is the mechanical work from the hand of man, that can compare with this lofty tree whose trunk, now laden with branches, slept not long since buried in an imperceptible germ? Does not one perceive that this mighty tree, which at first, weak blade of grass, pierced with difficulty the ground which concealed its principles, can in nowise be considered as the production of a blind and capricious force, but on the contrary, as that of wisdom enlightened and steadfast in its designs? Now speech is like this majestic tree; it has its germ, it spreads its roots gradually in a fertile nature whose elements are unknown, it breaks its bonds and rises upward escaping from terrestrial darkness and bursts forth into new regions where, breathing a purer element, watered by a divine light, it spreads its branches and covers them with flowers and fruit.

But perhaps the objection will be made that this comparison which could not be questioned for Hebrew, whose successive developments I have amply demonstrated, is limited to this tongue, and that it would be in vain for me to attempt the same labour for another. I reply, that this objection, to have any force must be as affirmative as is my proof, instead of being negative; that is to say, that instead of saying to me that I have not done it, it is still to be done; he must demonstrate to me, for example, that French, Latin or Greek are so constituted that they can not be brought back to their principles, or what amounts to the same thing, to the primordial signs upon which the mass of words which compose them rest; a matter which I deny absolutely. The difficulty of the analysis of these idioms, I am convinced, is due to their complexity and remoteness from their origin; however, the analysis is by no means impossible. That of Hebrew, which now appears easy owing to the method I have followed, was none the less before this test, the stumbling-block of all etymologists. This tongue is very simple; its material offers advantageous results; but what would it be if the reasons which have led me to chose Hebrew had also inclined me toward Chinese! what a mine to exploit! what food for thought!

I return to the formation of the Hebraic verbs. I have shown in the preceding section that it was by the intermediary of the facultatives that the convertible sign ו׳ raised the noun to the dignity of the verb. It is essential that we examine what the idiomatic genius adds to this creation.

This genius affects particularly the words composed of three consonant characters; that is to say, words which come from a primitive root governed by a sign, or from two roots contracted and forming two syllables. It is this which has caused the superficial etymologists and those who receive things without examination, to believe that the tongue of the Hebrews was essentially dissyllabic and that its roots could consist only of three characters. Ridiculous error, which veiling the origin of the words, and confounding the auxiliary sign and even the article, with the root itself, has finally corrupted the primitive meaning and brought forth in Hebrew, a sort of jargon, wholly different from the Hebrew itself.

Primitive roots are, in all known tongues, monosyllabic. I cannot repeat this truth too strongly. The idiomatic genius can indeed, as in Hebrew, add to this syllable, either to modify its meaning or to reinforce its expression; but it can never denature it. When by the aid of the convertible sign ו, the nominal verb is formed, as I have said, it is formed either of the root, as can be seen in שׂוּם *to constitute, to put up, to decree;* or of the compound substantive מלוֹךְ *to rule*: but one feels the primitive root always, even in the nominal מלוֹךְ, when he is intellectually capable of feeling it, or when he is not fettered by grammatical prejudices. If the reader is curious to know what this root is, I will tell him that it is אךְ, and that the expansive sign ל, governs jointly with that of exterior and local action, מ. Now לאךְ, develops all idea of legation, of function to which one is linked: of vicariate, of mission, etc., thus the word מֶלֶךְ *a king,* the origin of which is Ethiopic, signifies properly, a delegate, an envoy absolute; a minister charged with representing the divinity on earth. This word has had in its origin, the same meaning as מַלְאָךְ, of which we have adopted the Greek translation ἄγγελος, *an angel*. The primitive root αγ, which forms the basis of the Greek word ἄγγελος, is precisely the same as the Hebraic root אך, and like it develops ideas of attachment and of legation. This root belongs to the tongue of the Celts as well as to that of the Ethiopians and the Hebrews. It has become, through nasalization, our idiomatic root *ang*, from which the Latins and all modern peoples generally, have received derivatives.

Taking up again the thread of my ideas, which this etymological digression has for a moment suspended, I repeat, that the Hebraic genius which is singularly partial to words of two syllables, rarely allows the verb to be formed of the root without adding a character which modifies the meaning or reinforces the expression. Now it is in the following manner that the adjunction is made and the characters especially consecrated to this use.

This adjunction is initial or terminative; that is to say, that the character added is placed at the beginning or the end of the word. When the adjunction is initial, the character added at the head of the root is י or נ; when it is terminative it is simply the final character which is doubled.

Let us take for example the verb שׂוֹם that I have already cited. This verb will become, by means of the initial adjunction יְשׂוֹם, or נְשׂוֹם, and by means of the terminative adjunction, שׂוֹמֵם: but then, not only will the meaning vary considerably and receive acceptations very different from the primitive meaning, but the conjugation also will appear irregular, on account of the characters having been added after the formation of the verb, and the root will not always be in evidence. The result of this confusion of ideas is that the Hebraists, devoid of all etymological science, take roots sometimes for radical verbs, relative to the new meaning which they offer, and sometimes for irregular verbs, relative to the anomalies that they experience in their modifications.

But the truth is, that these verbs are neither radical verbs nor irregular verbs: these are verbs of a kind, distinct and peculiar to the Hebraic tongue; verbs of which it is necessary to understand the origin and development, so as to distinguish them in speech and assign them a rank in grammar. I shall name them *compound radical* verbs, as holding a mean between those which come directly from the root and those which are formed from the derivative substantives.

I classify verbs in three kinds, with regard to conjugation, namely: the radical, the derivative and the compound radical. By the first, I mean those which are derived from the root and which remain monosyllables, such as שׁוֹם, בּוּל, גּוּל etc. By the second, those which are derived from a substantive already compound, and which are always dissyllables such as מָלוֹךְ, רָגוֹז, פָּקוֹד etc. By the third, those which are formed by the adjunction of an initial or terminative character to the root, and which appear in the course of the conjugation sometimes monosyllabic and sometime dissyllabic, such as יָשׁוֹם, שׁוֹמֵם, נָשׁוֹם etc.

§ III.

Analysis of Nominal Verbs: Verbal Inflection.

The signification of radical verbs depends always upon the idea attached to their root. When the etymologist has this root firmly in his memory, it is hardly possible for him to err in the meaning of the verb which is developed. If he knows well, for example, that the root שׁם contains the general idea of a thing, upright, straight, remarkable; of a monument, a name, a sign, a place, a fixed and determined time; he will know well that the verb שׁום, which is formed from it, must express the action of instituting, enacting, noting, naming, designating, placing, putting up, etc. according to the meaning of the context.

The compound radical verbs offer, it is true, a few more difficulties, for it is necessary to join to the etymological understanding of the root, that of the initial or terminative adjunction; but this is not impossible. The first step, after finding the root, is to conceive clearly the sort of influence that this same root and the character which is joined to it, exercise upon each other; for their action in this respect is reciprocal: here lies the only difficulty. The signification of the joined characters is not in the least perplexing. One must know that the characters ו and נ express, in their qualities as sign, the first, a potential manifestation, an intellectual duration, and the second, an existence, produced, dependent and passive. So that one can admit as a general underlying idea, that the adjunction ו, will give to the verbal action, an exterior force, more energetic and more durable, a movement more apparent and more determined; whereas the adjunction נ, on the contrary, will render this same action more interior and more involved, by bringing it back to itself.

As to the terminative adjunction, since it depends upon the duplication of the final sign, it also draws all its expression from this same sign whose activity it doubles.

But let us take as an example of these three modifications, the root שׁם, which we already know as radical verb, and let us consider it as compound radical verb. In taking this verb שׁום, in the sense of *setting up*, which is its simplest acceptation, we shall find that the initial adjunction manifesting its action, gives it in יׁשׁום, the sense of *exposing*, of *placing in sight*, of *putting in a prominent place:* but if this verb is presented in a more figurative sense as that of *elevating*, we shall see that the initial adjunction נ, bringing back its action in itself, makes it signify, *to elevate the soul, to be inspired, to be animated; to assume*, as it were, *the spirit of the loftiest and most radiant parts of universal spirituality.* These are the two initial adjunctions.

The terminative adjunction being formed by the duplication of the final character, it is expedient to examine this character in the root שׁם. Now, this character, considered as the sign of exterior action, is used here in its quality of collective sign. But this sign which already tends very much to extension, and which develops the being in infinite space as much as its nature permits, can not be doubled without reaching that limit where extremes meet. Therefore, the extension, of which it is the image, is changed to a dislocation, a sort of annihilation of being, caused by the very excess of its expansive action. Also the radical verb שׁום, which is limited to signifying the occupation of a distinguished, eminent place, presents in the compound radical שׁמם, only the action of *extending* in the void, of *wandering* in space, of *depriving of stability* of *making deserted*, of *being delirious*, etc.

In this manner should the radical and the compound radical verbs be analyzed. As to the derivative verbs, their analysis is no more difficult; for, as they come for the most part from a triliteral substantive, they receive from it verbal expression. I shall have many occasions for examining these sorts of verbs in the course of my notes upon the *Cosmogony of Moses*, so that I shall dispense with doing so here: nevertheless, in order to leave nothing to be desired, in this respect, for the reader who follows me closely, I shall give two examples.

Let us take two verbs of great importance. בָּרוֹא *to create* and אָמוֹר *to speak, to say, to declare*. The first thing to do is to bring them both back to the substantives from which they are derived: this is simply done, by taking away the sign וֹ, which verbalizes them. The former presents to me in ברא, the idea of an emanated production, since בר signifies *a son, an exterior fruit;* the latter, in אמר, *a declaration, a thing upon which light is thrown,* since מאר signifies a *luminous focus, a torch*. In the first, the character א is a sign of stability; in the second, it is only a transposition from the middle of the word to the beginning to give more energy. Let us take the first.

The word בר, considered as primitive root, signifies not only *a son,* but develops the general idea of every production emanated from a generative being. Its elements are worthy of the closest attention. It is on the other hand, the sign of movement proper ר, united to that of interior action ב. The first of these signs, when it is simply vocalized by the mother vowel א as in אר, is applied to the elementary principle, whatever it may be, and under whatever form it may be conceived; ethereal, igneous, ærial, aqueous or terrestrial principle. The second of these signs is preëminently the paternal symbol. Therefore the elementary principle, whatever it may be, moved by an interior, generative force, constitutes the root באר whence is formed the compound substantive בָּרָא and the verb that I am analyzing, ברוא: that is to say, *to draw from an unknown element; to make pass from the principle to the essence; to make same that which was other;*

to bring from the centre to the circumference; in short, *to create.*

Now let us see the word מאר. This word is supported likewise by the elementary root אר, but this root being enlightened by the intellectual sign וֹ, has become אוֹר *the light.* In this state it assumes, not the paternal sign בּ, as in the word ברא, that I have just examined, but the maternal sign מ, image of exterior action, so as to constitute the substantive מאר or מאוֹר: also, it is no longer an interior and creative action, but an action exterior and propagating, a *reflection;* that is to say, a luminous focus, a torch diffusing light from which it has received the principle.

Such is the image of speech. Such at least is the etymology of the Hebraic verb אָמוֹר, which is to say, *to spread abroad its light; to declare its thought, its will; to speak,* etc.

I have now shown how verbs are formed and analyzed; let us see how they are inflected with the aid of the designative relations which I have called articles. This inflection will prove that these verbs are really nominal, partaking, on the one hand, of the name from which they are derived by their substance, and on the other, of the absolute verb from which they receive the verbal life.

MOVEMENT.	*enunciative*	מְלוֹךְ	the action of ruling
	determinative	הַמְלוֹךְ	of the action of ruling
	directive	לִמְלוֹךְ	to the action of ruling
	extractive	מִמְלוֹךְ	from the action of ruling
	mediative	בִּמְלוֹךְ	in the action of ruling
	assimilative	כִּמְלוֹךְ	conformable to the action of ruling
	conjunctive	וּמְלוֹךְ	and the action of ruling
	designative	אֶת־מָלוֹךְ	that which constitutes the action of ruling

VERBAL INFLECTION

I have a very important observation to make concerning this verbal inflection. It is with regard to the conjunctive article וֹ. This article which, placed in front of the nominal verb, expresses only the conjunctive movement as in the above example, takes all the force of the convertible sign, before the future or past tense of this same verb, and changes their temporal modification in such a way that the future tense becomes past and the past tense takes all the character of the future. Thus for example the future יִהְיָה *it shall be*, changes abruptly the signification in receiving the conjunctive article וֹ, and becomes the past וַיְהִי *and it was*: thus the past הָיָה *it was*, loses too its original meaning in taking the same article וֹ, and becomes the future וְהָיָה *and it shall be*.

It is impossible to explain in a satisfactory manner this idiomatic Hebraism without admitting the intrinsic force of the universal, convertible sign וֹ and without acknowledging its influence in this case.

Besides, we have an adverbial relation in our own tongue, that exercises an action almost similar, upon a past tense, which it makes a future. I do not recall having seen this singular idiomatism pointed out by any grammarian. It is the adverbial relation *if*. I am giving this example to the reader that he may see in what manner a past can become a future, without the mind being disturbed by the boldness of the ellipsis and without it even striking the attention. *They were* is assuredly of the past; it becomes future in this phrase: if *they were* in ten years at the end of their labours they would be happy!

The nominal verb participating, as I have said, in two natures, adopts equally the nominal and verbal affixes. One finds מְלוֹכִי and מַלְכָּנִי *the action of ruling, mine* (my rule): מְלוֹכוֹ and מַלְכֵהוּ *the action of ruling, his* (his rule): etc.

One perceives that it is only the sense of the sentence which can indicate whether the affix added here is nominal or verbal. It is an amphibology that Hebrew writers would have been able to evade easily, by distinguishing the nominal affixes from the verbal.

Here is an example of the verbal and nominal affixes united to the nominal verb. I have followed the Chaldaic punctuation, which, always submissive to the vulgar pronunciation, replaces the verbal sign וֹ, on this occasion, by the weak vowel point, named *shewa*.

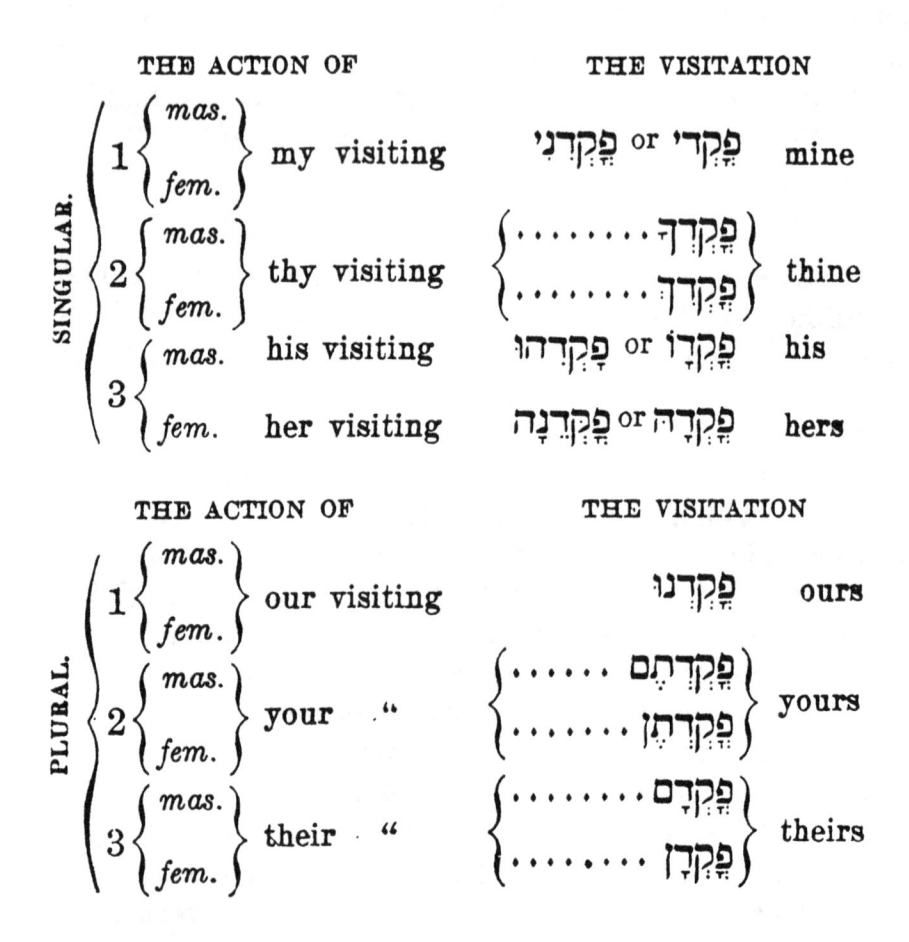

		THE ACTION OF		THE VISITATION	
SINGULAR.	1 { *mas.* / *fem.* }	my visiting	פָּקְדִי or פְּקָדְנִי	mine
	2 { *mas.* / *fem.* }	thy visiting	פָּקְדְךָ / פָּקְדֵךְ	thine
	3 { *mas.*	his visiting	פָּקְדוֹ or פְּקָדְהוּ	his
	fem.	her visiting	פָּקְדָהּ or פְּקָדְנָה	hers

		THE ACTION OF		THE VISITATION	
PLURAL.	1 { *mas.* / *fem.* }	our visiting	פָּקְדֵנוּ	ours
	2 { *mas.* / *fem.* }	your "	פְּקָדְתֶם / פְּקָדְתֶן	yours
	3 { *mas.* / *fem.* }	their "	פְּקָדָם / פְּקָדָן	theirs

CHAPTER VIII.

MODIFICATIONS OF THE VERB.

§ I.

Form and Movement.

In the preceding chapter I have spoken of the absolute verb, of the particular verbs which emanate from it, and of the various kinds of these verbs. I have stated that these verbs were subject to four modifications: form, movement, time and person. I am about to make known the nature of these modifications; afterward, I shall give models of the conjugations for all the kinds of verbs of the Hebraic tongue: for I conceive as many conjugations as I have kinds of verbs, namely: radical, derivative and compound radical conjugations. I do not know why the Hebraists have treated as irregular, the first and third of these conjugations, when it is obvious that one of them, the radical, is the type of all the others and particularly of the derivative, which they have chosen for their model in consequence of an absurd error which placed the triliteral verb in the first etymological rank.

I am beginning with an explanation of what ought to be understood by the *form* of the verb, and its *movement* which is here inseparable.

I call verbal form, that sort of modification by means of which the Hebraic verbs display an expression more or less forceful, more or less direct, more or less simple or compound. I recognize four verbal forms: positive, intensive, excitative and reflexive or reciprocal form.

The movement is active or passive. It is inherent in the form; for under whatever modification the verb may appear, it is indispensable that it present an active or passive action; that is to say, an action which exercises itself from within outwardly by an agent upon an object, or an action which exercises itself from without inwardly, by an object upon an agent. *One loves* or *one is loved; one sees* or *one is seen*, etc.

The verbs to which modern grammarians have given the somewhat vague name of *neuter verbs* and which appear indeed to be neither active nor passive, such as *to sleep, to walk, to fall, etc.*, are verbs, not which unite the two movements, as Harris[1] believed because this definition agrees only with the reflexive form; but verbs wherein the verbal action itself seizes the agent and suspends it between the two movements, making it object without taking from it any of its faculty of agent. Thus, when I say: *I sleep, I walk, I fall;* it is as if one said: *I devote myself to the action of sleeping, of walking, of falling, which now exercises itself upon me.* Far from having called these verbs *neuter,* that is to say, foreign to active and passive movement, the grammarians should have named them *superactives;* for they dominate the active movement, even as one has proof in considering that there is not a single active verb which, by an abstraction of thought, being taken in a general sense independent of any object, cannot take the character of the verbs in question. When one says, for example, *man loves, hates, wills, thinks,* etc., the verbs *to love, to hate, to will, to think* are in reality *superactives;* that is to say, that the verbal action which they express, dominates the agent and suspends in it the active movement, without in any manner rendering it passive.

But let us leave modern grammar which is not my domain and enter that of the Hebrews, to which I would confine myself. It is useless to speak of the superactive movement, which all verbs can take, which all can leave and which besides, differs in nothing from the active movement in its characteristic course. Let us limit ourselves to the two movements of which I have first spoken

---

[1] *Hermes,* L. I. c. 9.

and see how they are characterized according to their inherent form.

I call *positive,* the first of the four forms of Hebraic verbs. In this form the verbal action, active or passive, is announced simply and in accordance with its original nature. The passive movement is distinguished from the active by means of the two characters נ and ה; the first, which is the sign of produced being, governs the continued facultative; the second, which is that of life, governs the nominal verb. Therefore one finds for the active movement, קוֹם or קָם, *to be establishing,* קוֹם, *the action of establishing;* and for the passive movement נָקוֹם, *being established,* הקוֹם, *the action of being established.*

The second form is what I name *intensive,* on account of the intensity which it adds to the verbal action. Our modern tongues which are deprived of this form, supply the deficiency by the aid of modificatives. This form, which a speaker can use with great force, since the accent of the voice is able to give energetic expression, is very difficult to distinguish today in writing, particularly, since the Chaldaic punctuation has substituted for the mother vowel ׳, placed after the first character of the verb, the imperceptible point called *hirek*. The only means which remains to recognize this form, is the redoubling of the second verbal character, which being marked unfortunately again by the insertion of the interior point, is hardly more striking than the point *hirek*. The rabbis having recognized this difficulty have assumed the very wise part of giving to the mother vowel ׳, the place which has been taken from it by this last mentioned point. It would perhaps be prudent to imitate them, for this form which is of the highest importance in the books of Moses, has scarcely ever been perceived by his translators. The active and passive facultative is governed by the character מ, sign of exterior action, and the second character is likewise doubled in both movements; but in the active movement, the nominal verb adopts the mother vowel י, or the point *hirek* after the first character; in the passive movement it takes the mother vowel ו, or the point *kibbuz*. For the active movement, one finds מְפַקֵּד, *to be visiting, inspecting with diligence:* פִּיקֵד or פַּקֵּד *the action of visiting*, etc.; for the passive movement מְפֻקָּד, *being visited, inspected with diligence:* פּוֹקוֹד or פֻּקוֹד, *the action of being visited*, etc.

I qualify the third form by the name of *excitative*, in order to make understood as much as possible, by one single word, the kind of excitation that it causes in the verbal action, transporting this action beyond the subject which acts, upon another which it is a question of making act. This form is of great effect in the tongue of Moses. Happily it has a character that the Chaldaic point has never been able to supply and which makes it easily recognized: it is the sign of life ה, which governs the nominal verb in the two movements. For the active movement מֵקִים *to be establishing;* הֵקֵם or הָקִים *the action of establishing*: and for passive movement מוּקָם *being established;* הוּקַם *the action of being established.*

The fourth form is that which I name *reciprocal* or *reflexive*, because it makes the verbal action reciprocal or because it reflects it upon the very subject which is acting. It is easily recognized by means of the characteristic syllable הת composed of the united signs of life and of reciprocity. The second character of the verb, is doubled in this form as in the intensive, thus conserving all the energy of the latter. The two movements are also here united in a single one, to indicate that the agent which makes the action, becomes the object of its own action. One finds for the continued facultative מִתְפַּקֵּד *visiting each other;* הִתְפַּקֵּד *the action of visiting each other.*

I shall now enter into some new details regarding these four forms in giving models of the conjugations.

§ II.

Tense.

Thus Hebraic verbs are modified with respect to form and movement. I hope that the attentive reader has not failed to observe with what prolific richness the principles, which I have declared to be those of the tongue of Moses in particular, and those of all tongues in general, are developed, and I hope it will not be seen without some interest, that the sign, after having furnished the material of the noun, becomes the very substance of the verb and influences its modifications. For, let him examine carefully what is about to be explained—two movements being united to four forms. One of these movements is passive, and from its origin, is distinguished from the active, by the sign of produced being. The form, if intensive, is the sign of the duration and the manifestation which constitutes it: if it is excitative, it is the same sign united to that of life: if it is reflexive, it is the sign of that which is reciprocal and mutual, which is presented. There is such a continuous chain of regularity that I cannot believe it is the result of chance.

Now, let us pass on to the different modifications of Hebraic verbs under the relation of Tense. If, before seeing what these modifications are, I should wish to examine, as Harris[1] and some other grammarians, the nature of this incomprehensible being which causes them,—Time, what trouble would I not experience in order to develop unknown ideas; ideas that I would be unable to sustain with anything sentient! for how can Time affect our material organs since *the past* is no more; since *the future* is not; since *the present* is contained in an indivisible in-

[1] *Hermes*, L. I. ch. 7.

stant? Time is an indecipherable enigma for whatever is contained within the circle of the sensations, and nevertheless the sensations alone give it a relative existence. If they did not exist, what would it be?

It is measure of life. Change life and you will change Time. Give another movement to matter and you will have another space. Space and Time are analogous things. There, it is matter which is changed; here, it is life. Man, intelligent and sentient being, understands matter through his corporeal organs, but not through those of his intelligence; he has the intellectual sentiment of life, but he grasps it not. This is why Space and Time which appear so near, remain unknown to him. In order to understand them, man must needs awaken a third faculty within him, which being supported at the same time both by sensations and by sentiment, and enlightening at the same time the physical and mental qualities, unites in them the separated faculties. Then a new universe would be unveiled before his eyes; then he would fathom the depths of space, he would grasp the fugitive essence of Time; it would be known in its double nature.

Still if one asks me if this third faculty exists, or even if it can exist, I shall state that it is what Socrates called *divine inspiration* and to which he attributed the power of virtue.

But whatever Time may be, I have not dwelt a moment upon its nature, I have only tried to make its profound obscurity felt, in order that it be understood, that all peoples, not having considered it in the same manner, could not have experienced the same effects. Also it is very necessary in all idioms, that verbs conform to the tenses, and especially that the idiomatic genius should assign them the same limits.

The modern tongues of Europe are very rich in this respect, but they owe this richness, first, to the great number of idioms whose *débris* they have collected and of which they were insensibly composed; afterward, with the progress of the mind of man whose ideas, accumulating with the centuries, are refined and polished more and more, and are developed into a state of perfection. It is a matter worthy of notice, and which holds very closely to the history of mankind, that the tongues of the North of Europe, those whence are derived the idioms so rich today in temporal modifications, had in their origin only two simple tenses, the *present* and the *past*: they lacked the future; whereas the tongues of Occidental Asia, which appear of African origin, lacked the present, having likewise only two simple tenses, the *past* and the *future*.

Modern grammarians who have broached the delicate question of the number of tenses possessed by the French tongue, one of the most varied of Europe, and of the world in this regard, have been very far from being in accord. Some have wished to recognize only five, counting as real tenses, only the simplest ones, such as *I love, I loved, I was loving, I shall love, I should love;* considering the others as but temporal gradations. Abbé Girard has enumerated eight; Harris, twelve; Beauzée, twenty. These writers instead of throwing light upon this matter have obscured it more and more. They are like painters who, with a palette charged with colours, instead of instructing themselves or instructing others concerning their usage and the best manner of mixing them, amuse themselves disputing over their number and their rank.

There are three principal colours in light, as there are three principal tenses in the verb. The art of painting consists in knowing how to distinguish these principal colours, *blue, red* and *yellow;* the median colours *violet, orange* and *green;* and those median colours of infinite shades which can arise from their blending. Speech is a means of painting thought. The tenses of the verb are the coloured lights of the picture. The more the palette is rich in shades, the more a people gives flight to its imagination. Each writer makes use of this palette according to his genius. It is in the delicate manner of composing the shades and of mixing them, that painters and writers are alike distinguished.

It is well known that ancient painters were ignorant of the shades and half-tones. They used the primary colours without mixing them. A picture composed of four colours was regarded as a miracle of art. The colours of speech were not more varied. These shades of verbal light which we call compound tenses were unknown. The Hebrews were not poorer in this respect, than the Ethiopians and the Egyptians, renowned for their wisdom; the Assyrians, famous for their power; the Phœnicians, recognized for their vast discoveries and their colonies; the Arabs finally, whose high antiquity can not be contested: all of these had, properly speaking, only two verbal tenses: the *future* and the *past*.

But one must not think that in these ancient tongues, and particularly in the Hebrew, these two tenses were so determined, so decisive, as they have since become in our modern idioms, or that they signified precisely that which was, or that which must be, as we understand by *it has been, it shall be;* the temporal modifications הָיָה, and יִהְיֶה, express in Hebrew, not a rupture, a break in temporal continuity, but a continued duration, uniting, without the slightest interruption, the most extreme point of the past to the indivisible instant of the present, and this indivisible instant to the most extreme point of the future. So that it was sufficient by a single restriction of thought, by a simple inflection of the voice, to fix upon this temporal line, any point whatever from the past to the present, or from the present to the future, and to obtain thus by the aid of the two words הָיָה and יִהְיֶה, the same differences which modern tongues acquire with difficulty, through the following combinations: *I was, I have been, I had been, I shall be, I should be, I may have been, I might have been, I ought to be, I would be, I have to be, I had to be, I am about to be, I was about to be.*

I have purposely omitted from this list of **tenses** the indivisible instant *I am,* which makes the fourteenth, because this instant is never expressed in Hebrew except by the pronoun alone, or by the continued facultative, as in אָנֹכִי יְהוָֹה, *I am* YAHWEH: הִנְנִי מֵבִיא *behold me leading;* etc.

It is on this account that one should be careful in a correct translation, not always to express the Hebraic past or future, which are vague tenses, by the definite tenses. One must first examine the intention of the writer, and the respective condition of things. Thus, to give an example, although, in the French and English *word-for-word* translation, conforming to custom, I have rendered the verb בָּרָא, of the first verse of the Cosmogony of Moses, by *he created,* I have clearly felt that this verb signified there, *he had created;* as I have expressed it in the correct translation; for this antecedent nuance is irresistibly determined by the verb הָיְתָה, *it existed,* in speaking of the earth an evident object of an anterior creation.

Besides the two tenses of which I have just spoken, there exists still a third tense in Hebrew, which I call *transitive,* because it serves to transport the action of the past to the future, and because it thus participates in both tenses by serving them as common bond. Modern grammarians have improperly named it *imperative.* This name would be suitable if used only to express commands; but as one employs it as often in examining, desiring, demanding and even entreating, I do not see why one should refuse it a name which would be applicable to all these ideas and which would show its transitive action.

§ III.

Formation of Verbal Tenses by Means of Pronominal Persons.

After having thus made clear the modification of Hebraic verbs relative to tense, there remains only for me to say how they are formed. But before everything else it is essential to remember what should be understood by the three Pronominal Persons.

When I treated of nominal relations, known under the denomination of Personal and Relative pronouns, I did not stop to explain what should be understood by the three Pronominal Persons, deeming that it was in speaking of the verb that these details would be more suitably placed, so much the more as my plan was to consider *person*, as one of the four modifications of the verb.

Person and tense are as inseparable as form and movement; never can the one appear without the other; for it is no more possible to conceive person without tense, than verbal form without active or passive movement.

At the time when I conceived the bold plan of bringing back the Hebraic tongue to its constitutive principles by deriving it wholly from the *sign*, I saw that the sign had three natural elements: *voice, gesture* and *traced characters*. Now by adhering to the traced characters to develop the power of the sign, I think I have made it clearly understood, that I consider them not as any figures whatever, denuded of life and purely material, but as symbolic and living images of the generative ideas of language, expressed at first by the sundry inflections which the voice received from the organs of man. Therefore these characters have always represented to me, the voice, by means of the verbal inflections whose symbols they are; they have also represented to me, the gesture with which each inflection is necessarily accompanied, and when the sign has developed the three parts of speech, the noun, the relation and the verb, although there may not be a single one of these parts where the three elements of speech do not act together, I have been able to distinguish, nevertheless, that part where each of them acts more particularly. The voice, for example, appears to me to be the dominant factor in the verb; the vocal accent or the character in the noun, and the gesture finally in the relation. So that if man making use of speech follows the sentiment of nature he must raise the voice in the verb, accentuate more the noun and place the gesture upon the relation. It seems even as though experience confirms this grammatical remark especially in what concerns the gesture. The article and the prepositions which are designative relations, the pronouns of any kind which are nominal relations, the adverbs which are adverbial relations, always involve a gesture expressed or understood. Harris had already observed this coincidence of the gesture and had not hesitated to place in it the source of all pronouns, following in this the doctrine of the ancients, related by Apollonius and Priscian.[1]

Harris was right in this. It is the gesture which, always accompanying the nominal relations, has given birth to the distinction of the three persons, showing itself by turn identical, mutual, other or relative. The identical gesture produces the first person *I*, or *me*, אֲנִי: this is a being which manifests itself; the mutual gesture produces the second person, *thou* or *thee* אַתָּה: this is a mutual being; the other, or relative gesture, produces the third per-

[1] *Hermes*. Liv. I. Chap. 5 Apoll. de *Synt*., Liv. II, Chap 5. Prisc. Liv. XII.

son, *he* or *him*. הוּא: this is another being, sometimes relative, as in the English pronoun, sometimes absolute, as in the Hebraic pronoun.

These personal pronouns whose origin I here explain, are like the substantive nouns which they replace in speech, subject to gender, number and inflection of the articles. I have explained them under these different relations and now we can see how in Hebrew, they determine the tense of the verbs. It is a matter worthy of attention and it has not escaped the sagacity of Court de Gébelin.[2] After being contracted in such a manner as not to be confused with the verbal affixes, the personal pronouns are placed before the nominal verb, when it is a question of forming the future, and to form the past, they are placed after the verb so as to express by this, that the action is already done.

By this simple yet energetic manner of showing verbal tenses, the Hebraic genius adds another which is none the less forceful and which proceeds from the power of the sign. It allows the luminous sign ו, which constitutes the nominal verb, to stand in the future; and not content with making it appear ו, in the finished facultative, makes it disappear wholly in the past; so that the third person of this tense, which is found without the masculine pronoun, is exactly the same as the root, or the compound whence the verb is derived. This apparent simplicity is the reason why the Hebraists have taken generally the third person of the past, for the root of the Hebraic verb and why they have given it this rank in all the dictionaries. Their error is having confounded the moment when it finishes, with that in which it begins, and not having had enough discernment to see that if the nominal verb

[2] *Grammaire Univ.* page 245. Court de Gébelin has put some obscurity into his explanation; but although he may be mistaken in respect to the tenses, it is plainly seen that what he said is exactly what I say.

FORMATION OF VERBAL TENSES 195

did not claim priority over all the tenses, this priority would belong to the transitive as the most simple of all.

Here is the new character which the personal pronouns take in order to form verbal tenses.

The affixes of the future placed before the verb, with the terminations which follow them.

SINGULAR.
- 1 { mas. / fem. } .... א I
- 2 { mas. .... תֹ / fem. ....תֹ׳ } thou
- 3 { mas. ....׳ he / fem. ....ת she }

PLURAL.
- 1 { mas. / fem. } ....נ we
- 2 { mas. ת...וֹ / fem. ת..נה } ye
- 3 { mas. ...וֹ..׳ / fem. ת..נה } they

Affixes of the past placed after the verb.

SINGULAR.
- 1 { mas. / fem. } ...תִּי I
- 2 { mas. ....תָּ / fem. ....תְּ } thou
- 3 { mas. ...... he / fem. ....ָה she }

PLURAL.
- 1 { mas. / fem. } ....נוּ we
- 2 { mas. ...תֶּם / fem. ....תֶּן } ye
- 3 { mas. / fem. } ......וּ they

I do not speak of the affixes of the transitive, because this tense, which holds a sort of mean between the future and the past, has no affixes properly speaking, but has terminations which it borrows from both tenses.

Hebraic words moreover, do not recognize what we call verbal moods, by means of which we represent in our modern idioms, the state of the will relative to the verbal action, whether that will is influential or resolute, as in *I am doing, I have done, I shall do;* whether it is dubitative or irresolute, as in *I might have done, I should have done, I would do;* or whether it is influenced or constrained, as in *I must do, that I may do; I was obliged to do, that I might have done; I shall be obliged to do; I should be obliged to do;* the modern tongue is of an inexhaustible richness in this respect. It colours with the most delicate shades all the volitive and temporal modifications of verbs. The nominal verb and also the transitive show this fine shading of the meaning. *To do,* for example, is an indefinite nominal, but *I have just done, I am doing, I am going to do,* show the same nominal expression of the past, the present and the future. The transitive *do,* conveys visibly the action from one tense to the other, but if I say *may have done, may have to do,* this change marks first a past in a future, and afterward a future in a future.

After this data I now pass on to the models of the three verbal conjugations, according to their forms and their movements, supporting them with certain remarks concerning the most striking anomalies which can be found.

CHAPTER IX.

Conjugations.

§ I.

Radical Conjugation.

Positive Form.

ACTIVE MOVEMENT.
CONTINUED FACULTATIVE

mas. קָם or קוֹם } to be
fem. קוֹמָה } establishing

PASSIVE MOVEMENT.
CONTINUED FACULTATIVE

mas. נְקוֹם } being
fem. נְקוֹמָה } established

FINISHED.

mas. קוֹם } to be established
fem. קוֹמָה }

NOMINAL VERB.

absol. קוֹם } to establish: action
constr. קוֹם } of establishing

absol. } הקוֹם } action of being
constr. } established

TEMPORAL VERB. FUTURE.

SINGULAR	1	m./f.	אָקוּם	I shall or will establish
	2	m.	תָּקוּם	thou shalt establish
		f.	תָּקוּמִי	
	3	m.	יָקוּם	he shall establish
		f.	תָּקוּם	she " "
PLURAL	1	m./f.	נָקוּם	we shall or will establish
	2	m.	תָּקוּמוּ	you shall establish
		f.	תָּקוּמֶנָה	
	3	m.	יָקוּמוּ	they shall establish
		f.	תָּקוּמֶנָה	
SINGULAR	1	m./f.	אֶקּוֹם	I shall or will be established
	2	m.	תִּקּוֹם	thou shalt be established
		f.	תִּקּוֹמִי	
	3	m.	יִקּוֹם	he shall be established
		f.	תִּקּוֹם	she " " "
PLURAL	1	m./f.	נִקּוֹם	we shall or will be established
	2	m.	תִּקּוֹמוּ	you shall be established
		f.	תִּקּוֹמֶנָה	
	3	m.	יִקּוֹמוּ	they shall be established
		f.	תִּקּוֹמֶנָה	

CONJUGATIONS

TRANSITIVE.

SING.	2	m.	קוּם	} establish
		f.	קוּמִי	
PLU.	2	m.	קוּמוּ	} establish
		f.	קוּמְנָה	
SING.	2	m.	הִקּוֹם	} be established
		f.	הִקּוֹמִי	
PLU.	2	m.	הִקּוֹמוּ	} be established
		f.	הִקּוֹמְנָה	

PAST.

SINGULAR.	1	m. / f.	קַמְתִּי	I established
	2	m.	קַמְתָּ	} thou established
		f.	קַמְתְּ	
	3	m.	קָם	he established
		f.	קָמָה	she "
PLURAL.	1	m. / f.	קַמְנוּ	we established
	2	m.	קַמְתֶּם	} you established
		f.	קַמְתֶּן	
	3	m. / f.	קָמוּ	they established

SINGULAR	1	m. f.	נְקוּמוֹתִי	I was established
	2	m.	נְקוּמוֹתָ	thou wast established
		f.	נְקוּמוֹת	
	3	m.	נָקוֹם	he was established
		f.	נָקוֹמָה	she " "
PLURAL	1	m. f.	נְקוּמוֹנוּ	we were established
	2	m.	נְקוּמוֹתָם	you were established
		f.	נְקוּמוֹתֶן	
	3	m. f.	נָקוֹמוּ	they were established

Intensive Form.

ACTIVE MOVEMENT.	PASSIVE MOVEMENT.

FACULTATIVE.

	CONTINUED.			CONTINUED.
mas.	מְקוֹמֵם		mas.	מְקוֹמָם
fem.	מְקוֹמְמָה		fem.	מְקוֹמְמָה

FINISHED.

mas. ....
fem. .... } like the passive

NOMINAL VERB.

| | absol.
constr. } | קוֹמֵם | | absol.
constr. } | קוֹמָם |

CONJUGATIONS

TEMPORAL VERB. FUTURE.

SINGULAR.	1	*m.* / *f.*	אָקוּםֶ	1	*m.* / *f.*	אָקוּםַ
	2	*m.*	תִּקוּםֶ	2	*m.*	תִּקוּםַ
		f.	תִּקוּמִי		*f.*	תִּקוּמִי
	3	*m.*	יִקוּםֶ	3	*m.*	יִקוּםַ
		f.	תִּקוּםֶ		*f.*	תִּקוּםַ
PLURAL.	1	*m.* / *f.*	נִקוּםֶ	1	*m.* / *f.*	נִקוּםַ
	2	*m.*	תִּקוּמוּ	2	*m.*	תִּקוּמוּ
		f.	תִּקוּמְנָה		*f.*	תִּקוּמַמְנָה
	3	*m.*	יִקוּמוּ	3	*m.*	יִקוּמוּ
		f.	תִּקוּמְנָה		*f.*	תִּקוּמַמְנָה

TRANSITIVE.

SING.	2	*m.*	קוּםֶ	2	*m.*	
		f.	קוּמִי		*f.*	} wanting
PLU.	2	*m.*	קוּמוּ	2	*m.*	
		f.	קוּמְנָה		*f.*	

PAST.

SINGULAR.	1	*m.* / *f.*	קוּמְתִּי	1	*m.* / *f.*	קוּמְתִּי
	2	*m.*	קוּמְתָּ	2	*m.*	קוּמְתָּ
		f.	קוּמְתְּ		*f.*	קוּמְתְּ
	3	*m.*	קוּםֶ	3	*m.*	קוּםַ
		f.	קוּמָה		*f.*	קוּמָה

$$\text{PLURAL} \begin{cases} 1 \begin{cases} m. \\ f. \end{cases} & \text{קוֹמַמְנוּ} \\ 2 \begin{cases} m. \\ f. \end{cases} & \begin{matrix} \text{קוֹמַמְתֶּם} \\ \text{קוֹמַמְתֶּן} \end{matrix} \\ 3 \begin{cases} m. \\ f. \end{cases} & \text{קוֹמְמוּ} \end{cases} \qquad \text{PLURAL} \begin{cases} 1 \begin{cases} m. \\ f. \end{cases} & \text{קוֹמַמְנוּ} \\ 2 \begin{cases} m. \\ f. \end{cases} & \begin{matrix} \text{קוֹמַמְתֶּם} \\ \text{קוֹמַמְתֶּן} \end{matrix} \\ 3 \begin{cases} m. \\ f. \end{cases} & \text{קוֹמְמוּ} \end{cases}$$

EXCITATIVE FORM.

ACTIVE MOVEMENT.   **PASSIVE MOVEMENT.**

FACULTATIVE.

CONTINUED.   CONTINUED.

mas. מֵקִים   *mas.* מוּקָם

fem. מְקִימָה   *fem.* מוּקָמָה

FINISHED.

mas. .... ⎫
fem. .... ⎬ like the passive

NOMINAL VERB.

absol. הָקֵם   *absol.* ⎫
constr. הָקִים   *constr.* ⎬ הוּקַם

CONJUGATIONS

TEMPORAL VERB.

FUTURE.

SINGULAR	1 {m./f.}	אָקִים		SINGULAR	1 {m./f.}	אוּקַם
	2 {m.}	תָּקִים			2 {m.}	תּוּקַם
	2 {f.}	תָּקִימִי			2 {f.}	תּוּקְמִי
	3 {m.}	יָקִים			3 {m.}	יוּקַם
	3 {f.}	תָּקִים			3 {f.}	תּוּקַם
PLURAL	1 {m./f.}	נָקִים		PLURAL	1 {m./f.}	נוּקַם
	2 {m.}	תָּקִימִי			2 {m.}	תּוּקְמוּ
	2 {f.}	תְּקִימֶינָה			2 {f.}	תּוּקַמְנָה
	3 {m.}	יָקִימוּ			3 {m.}	יוּקְמוּ
	3 {f.}	תְּקִימְנָה			3 {f.}	תּוּקַמְנָה

TRANSITIVE.

SING.	2 {m.}	הָקֵם		SING.	2 {m. ...... / f. ......}	
	2 {f.}	הָקִימִי				wanting
PLU.	2 {m.}	הָקִימוּ		PLU.	2 {m. ...... / f. ......}	
	2 {f.}	הָקֵמְנָה				

PAST.

SINGULAR	1	m. f.	הֲקִימוֹתִי	SINGULAR	1	m. f.	הוּקַמְתִּי
	2	m.	הֲקִימוֹתָ		2	m.	הוּקַמְתָּ
		f.	הֲקִימוֹתְ			f.	הוּקַמְתְּ
	3	m.	הֵקִים		3	m.	הוּקַם
		f.	הֵקִימָה			f.	הוּקְמָה
PLURAL	1	m. f.	הֲקִימוֹנוּ	PLURAL	1	m. f.	הוּקַמְנוּ
	2	m.	הֲקִימוֹתֶם		2	m.	הוּקַמְתֶּם
		f.	הֲקִימוֹתֶן			f.	הוּקַמְתֶּן
	3	m. f.	הֵקִימוּ		3	m. f.	הוּקְמוּ

REFLEXIVE FORM.

ACTIVE AND PASSIVE MOVEMENT UNITED.

FACULTATIVE.

CONTIN. { mas. מִתְקוֹמֵם
         { fem. מִתְקוֹמְמָה

FINISH. { mas. .... }
        { fem. .... } wanting

CONJUGATIONS

NOMINAL VERB.

FUTURE.

absol. ⎫
constr. ⎬ הִתְקוֹמֵם

TEMPORAL VERB.

FUTURE.

SINGULAR.
- 1 { *mas.* / *fem.* } אֶתְקוֹמֵם
- 2 *mas.* תִּתְקוֹמֵם
- 2 *fem.* תִּתְקוֹמְמִי
- 3 *mas.* יִתְקוֹמֵם
- 3 *fem.* תִּתְקוֹמֵם

PLURAL.
- 1 { *mas.* / *fem.* } נִתְקוֹמֵם
- 2 *mas.* תִּתְקוֹמְמוּ
- 2 *fem.* תִּתְקוֹמֵמְנָה
- 3 *mas.* יִתְקוֹמְמוּ
- 3 *fem.* תִּתְקוֹמֵמְנָה

TRANSITIVE

SING.	2	*mas.*	הִתְקוֹמֵם
		fem.	הִתְקוֹמְמִי
PLU.	2	*mas.*	הִתְקוֹמְמוּ
		fem.	הִתְקוֹמֵמְנָה

PAST.

SINGULAR	1	*mas.* / *fem.*	הִתְקוֹמַמְתִּי
	2	*mas.*	הִתְקוֹמַמְתָּ
		fem.	הִתְקוֹמַמְתְּ
	3	*mas.*	הִתְקוֹמֵם
		fem.	הִתְקוֹמֵמָה
PLURAL	1	*mas.* / *fem.*	הִתְקוֹמַמְנוּ
	2	*mas.*	הִתְקוֹמַמְתֶּם
		fem.	הִתְקוֹמַמְתֶּן
	3	*mas.* / *fem.*	הִתְקוֹמְמוּ

Remarks upon the Radical Conjugation.

I have already clearly shown why the conjugation which the Hebraists treat as irregular, should be considered as the first of all. The verbs which depend upon it are those which are formed directly from the root. The one that I have chosen as type is the same as that which the Hebraists have ordinarily chosen. As to the meaning, it is one of the most difficult of all the Hebraic tongue. The Latin *surgere* expresses only the least of its acceptations. As I shall often have occasion to speak of it in my notes, I am limiting myself to one simple analysis.

The sign ק is, as we know, the sign of agglomerative or repressive force, the image of material existence, the means of the forms. Now this sign offers a different expression according as it begins or terminates the root. If it terminates it as in חק, for example, it characterizes that which is finished, definite, bound, arrested, cut, shaped upon a model, designed: if it begins it, as in קה, קו or קי, it designates that which is indefinite, vague, indeterminate, unformed. In the first case it is matter put in action; in the second, it is matter appropriate to be put in action. This last root, bearing in the word קום or קים, the collective sign, represents *substance* in general; employed as verb it expresses all the ideas which spring from substance and from its modifications: such as, *to substantialize, to spread out, to rise into space; to exist in substance, to subsist, to consist, to resist; to clothe in form and in substance, to establish, to constitute, to strengthen, to make firm*, etc. One must feel after this example, how difficult and dangerous it is to confine the Hebraic verbs to a fixed and determined expression; for this expression results always from the meaning of the phrase and the intention of the writer.

As to the four forms to which I here submit the verb קום, I must explicitly state, not only as regards this conjugation but also for those which follow, that all verbs do not receive them indifferently; that some affect one form more than another, and finally, that there are some which one never finds under the positive form. But once again, what matter these variations? It is not a question of writing but of understanding Hebrew.

Positive Form.

Active movement. Although the modern Hebraists, with an unprecedented whimsicality, have taken the third person of the past for the theme of all verbs, they are forced to agree that in this conjugation, this third person is not in the least thematic: one also finds in dictionaries, the nominal קוּם presented as theme: and this ought to be, not only for all radical verbs such as this one, but for all kinds of verbs.

The continued facultative is often marked by the luminous, sign וֹ, as can be seen in אוֹר *to be shining*. The Chaldaic punctuation is not consistent in the manner of replacing this sign: Instead of the point *kamez* which is found here in קָם, one meets the *zere*, in עֵר *to be watching, vigilant,* and in some others. I state here once more, that the feminine facultative, in the continued active and passive, as well as in the finished, changes the character הָ into ת, and that one finds equally קוֹמָה or קוֹמֶת; נְקוֹמָה or נְקוֹמֶת; קוֹמָה or קוֹמֶת. I have already mentioned this variation in chapter V. § 3, in treating of gender. I do not mention the plural of the facultatives, since its formation offers no difficulties.

The future has sometimes the emphatic article ה, as well as the transitive. One finds אָקוֹמָה, *I shall establish, I shall raise up.* שׁוּבָה, *come! arise! return to thy first state,* etc.

The past, which, by its nature, ought to lose the luminous sign, conserves it, however, in certain verbs where it is identical; such as אוֹר, *it shone;* בּוּשׁ, *it reddened,* etc. One also finds the *zere* substituted by the *kamez* in מָת *he died.* I observe at this point, that all verbs in general which terminate with ת, do not double this character, either in the first or second person of the past, but receive the interior point only as duplicative accent. One finds therefore מַתִּי *I was dying,* מַתָּ *thou wast dying,* מַתֶּם *you were dying,* etc.

Passive movement. The inadequate denomination which the Hebraists had given to the facultatives in considering them as *present* or *past* participles, had always prevented them from distinguishing the continued facultative of the passive movement, from the finished facultative belonging to the two movements. It was impossible in fact, after their explanations to perceive the delicate difference which exists in Hebrew between נָקוֹם *that which became, becomes or will become established,* and קוּם, *that which was, is or will be established.* When, for example, it was a matter of explaining how the verb הָיוֹה or הֱיוֹת *the action of being, of living,* could have a passive facultative, they are lost in ridiculous interpretations. They perceived not that the difference of these three facultatives הוֹיָה, נִהְיָה and הָיוֹה was in the continued or finished movement: as we would say *a being being, living; a thing being effected; a being realized, a thing effected.*

It is easy to see, moreover, in the inspection of the passive movement alone, that the Chaldaic punctuation has altered it much less than the other. The verbal sign is almost invariably found in its original strength.

Intensive Form.

Radical verbs take this form by redoubling the final character; so that its signification depends always upon the signification of this character as sign. In the case in question, the final character being considered as collective sign, its redoubling expresses a sudden and general usurpation. Thus the verb קֹמֵם, can be translated, according to the circumstance, by the action of *extending indefinitely, of existing in substance in an universal manner; of establishing, of establishing strongly, with energy; of resisting, of opposing vigorously*, etc.

In this state this verb is easily confused with a derivative verb, if the verbal sign, instead of being placed after the first character, as it is, was placed after the second, as is seen in פָּקוֹד *to visit*: notwithstanding this difference, the rabbis, not finding this form sufficiently characterized, have substituted for it the hyphen of the Chaldaic, some examples of which, one finds moreover, in the Sepher of the Hebrews. This form consists in substituting the sign of manifestation and duration, for that of light, and in saying, without doubling the final character, קִים instead of קוֹמֵם; חַית instead of חוֹבֵב, etc.

Sometimes too, not content with doubling the last character of the root as in קוֹמֵם, the entire root is doubled, as in כִּלְכֵּל *to achieve, to consummate wholly*; but these sorts of verbs belong to the second conjugation and follow the intensive form of the derivative verbs.

The passive movement has nothing remarkable in itself except the very great difficulty of distinguishing it from the active movement, which causes it to be little used.

Excitative Form.

This form perfectly characterized, as much in the passive movement as in the active, is of great usefulness in the tongue of Moses. I have already spoken of its effects and of its construction. It can be observed in this example that the convertible sign ו, which constitutes the radical verb קוֹם, is changed into י, in the active movement, and is transposed in the passive movement, before the initial character.

The only comment I have to make is, that the Chal-

CONJUGATIONS

daic punctuation sometimes substitutes the point *zere* for the mother vowel ִי of the active movement, and the point *kibbuz* for the sign וּ of the passive movement. So that one finds the continued facultative מַכֵּר *making angry;* the future תָּשֵׁב, *thou shalt bring back,* and even the past הֻקַם, *he was aroused to establish himself;* etc.

Reflexive Form.

This form differs from the intensive in its construction, only by the addition of the characteristic syllable הִת; as can be seen in the nominal הִתְקוֹמֵם. For the rest, the two movements are united in a single one.

All that is essential to observe, is relative to this syllable הִת. Now it undergoes what the Hebraists call *syncope* and *metathesis*.

The syncope takes place when one of the two characters is effaced as in the facultative מִתְקוֹמֵם, and in the future אֶתְקוֹמֵם, where the character ה is found replaced by מ or א; or when, to avoid inconsonance, one supresses the character ת, before a verb commencing with ט, which takes its place with the interior point; as in תִּטָהֵר *to be purified*.

The metathesis takes place when the first character of a verb is one of the four following: ז, ס, צ, שׁ. Then the ת of the characteristic syllable הת, is transposed after this initial character, by being changed into ד after ז, and into ט after צ; as can be seen in the derivative verbs cited in the examples.

שָׁבוֹהַ	to praise, to exhalt	הִשְׁתַּבֵּיהַ	to be praised
צָדוֹק	to be just	הִצְטַדִּיק	to be justified
סָגוֹר	to close	הִסְתַּגִיר	to be closed
זָמָן	to prepare	הִזְדַּמִין	to be prepared

§ II.

DERIVATIVE CONJUGATION — POSITIVE FORM

ACTIVE MOVEMENT — **PASSIVE MOVEMENT**

FACULTATIVE

CONTINUED.

mas. פּוֹקֵד — mas. נִפְקָד

fem. פּוֹקְדָה — fem. נִפְקָדָה

FINISHED.

mas. פָּקֵד — fem. פְּקוּדָה

NOMINAL VERB

absol. פָּקֹד — absol. הִפָּקֵד

constr. פְּקֹד — constr.

TEMPORAL VERB

FUTURE.

			Active				Passive
SINGULAR	1	m./f.	אֶפְקֹד	SINGULAR	1	m./f.	אֶפָּקֵד
	2	m.	תִּפְקֹד		2	m.	תִּפָּקֵד
		f.	תִּפְקְדִי			f.	תִּפָּקְדִי
	3	m.	יִפְקֹד		3	m.	יִפָּקֵד
		f.	תִּפְקֹד			f.	תִּפָּקֵד
PLURAL	1	m./f.	נִפְקוֹד	PLURAL	1	m./f.	נִפָּקֵד
	2	m.	תִּפְקְדוּ		2	m.	תִּפָּקְדוּ
		f.	תִּפְקוֹדְנָה			f.	תִּפָּקֵדְנָה
	3	m.	יִפְקְדוּ		3	m.	יִפָּקְדוּ
		f.	תִּפְקוֹדְנָה			f.	תִּפָּקֵדְנָה

CONJUGATIONS

TRANSITIVE

SING. 2	mas.	פְּקוֹד	SING. 2	mas.	הִפָּקֵד
	fem.	פִּקְדִי		fem.	הִפָּקְדִי
PLU. 2	mas.	פִּקְדוּ	PLU. 2	mas.	הִפָּקְדוּ
	fem.	פְּקוֹדְנָה		fem.	הִפָּקֵדְנָה

PAST

SINGULAR. 1	mas. / fem.	פָּקַדְתִּי	SINGULAR. 1	mas. / fem.	נִפְקַדְתִּי
2	mas.	פָּקַדְתָּ	2	mas.	נִפְקַדְתָּ
	fem.	פָּקַדְתְּ		fem.	נִפְקַדְתְּ
3	mas.	פָּקַד	3	mas.	נִפְקַד
	fem.	פָּקְדָה		fem.	נִפְקְדָה
PLURAL. 1	mas. / fem.	פָּקַדְנוּ	PLURAL. 1	mas. / fem.	נִפְקַדְנוּ
2	mas.	פְּקַדְתֶּם	2	mas.	נִפְקַדְתֶּם
	fem.	פְּקַדְתֶּן		fem.	נִפְקַדְתֶּן
3	mas. / fem.	פָּקְדוּ	3	mas. / fem.	נִפְקְדוּ

INTENSIVE FORM

ACTIVE MOVEMENT		PASSIVE MOVEMENT	

FACULTATIVE.

CONTINUED

mas.	מְפַקֵּד	mas.	מְפֻקָּד
fem.	מְפַקְּדָה	fem.	מְפֻקָּדָה

FINISHED

mas.	פֻּקַּד	fem.	פֻּקָּדָה

NOMINAL VERB

absol. ⎫		absol. ⎫	
constr. ⎭	פַּקֵּד	constr. ⎭	פֻּקוֹד

TEMPORAL VERB

FUTURE.

SINGULAR
1 { m. / f. }	אֲפַקֵּד	1 { m. / f. }	אֲפֻקַּד
2 { m. }	תְּפַקֵּד	2 { m. }	תְּפֻקַּד
2 { f. }	תְּפַקְּדִי	2 { f. }	תְּפֻקְּדִי
3 { m. }	יְפַקֵּד	3 { m. }	יְפֻקַּד
3 { f. }	תְּפַקֵּד	3 { f. }	תְּפֻקַּד

PLURAL
1 { m. / f. }	נְפַקֵּד	1 { m. / f. }	נְפֻקַּד
2 { m. }	תְּפַקְּדוּ	2 { m. }	תְּפֻקְּדוּ
2 { f. }	תְּפַקֵּדְנָה	2 { f. }	תְּפֻקַּדְנָה
3 { m. }	יְפַקְּדוּ	3 { m. }	יְפֻקְּדוּ
3 { f. }	תְּפַקֵּדְנָה	3 { f. }	תְּפֻקַּדְנָה

CONJUGATIONS 215

TRANSITIVE

SING. 2 { mas. פְּקֹד / fem. פִּקְדִי }
PLU. 2 { mas. פִּקְדוּ / 'fem. פְּקֹדְנָה }

SING. 2 { mas. ...... / fem. ...... }
PLU. 2 { mas. ...... / fem. ...... } wanting

PAST

SINGULAR
1 { mas. / fem. } פָּקַדְתִּי
2 { mas. } פָּקַדְתָּ
  { fem. } פָּקַדְתְּ
3 { mas. } פָּקַד
  { fem. } פָּקְדָה

PLURAL
1 { mas. / fem. } פָּקַדְנוּ
2 { mas. } פְּקַדְתֶּם
  { fem. } פְּקַדְתֶּן
3 { mas. / fem. } פָּקְדוּ

SINGULAR
1 { mas. / fem. } פָּקַדְתִּ
2 { mas. } פָּקַדְתָּ
  { fem. } פָּקַדְתְּ
3 { mas. } פָּקַד
  { fem. } פָּקְדָה

PLURAL
1 { mas. / fem. } פָּקַדְנוּ
2 { mas. } פְּקַדְתֶּם
  { fem. } פְּקַדְתֶּן
3 { mas. / fem. } פָּקְדוּ

EXCITATIVE FORM

| ACTIVE MOVEMENT | PASSIVE MOVEMENT |

FACULTATIVE

CONTINUED

mas.	מַפְקִיד	mas.	מָפְקָד
fem.	מַפְקִידָה	fem.	מָפְקָדָה

FINISHED

mas. ..... ⎫
fem. ..... ⎬ like the passive

NOMINAL VERB

| absol. | הַפְקֵד | absol. | ⎫ הָפְקֵד |
| constr. | הַפְקִיד | constr. | ⎭ |

TEMPORAL VERB

FUTURE

SINGULAR

1	mas. / fem.	אַפְקִיד	1	mas. / fem.	אָפְקַד
2	mas.	תַּפְקִיד	2	mas.	תָּפְקַד
	fem.	תַּפְקִידִי		fem.	תָּפְקְדִי
3	mas.	יַפְקִיד	3	mas.	יָפְקַד
	fem.	תַּפְקִיד		fem.	תָּפְקַד

PLURAL

1	mas. / fem.	נַפְקִיד	1	mas. / fem.	נָפְקַד
2	mas.	תַּפְקִידוּ	2	mas.	תָּפְקְדוּ
	fem.	תַּפְקֵדְנָה		fem.	תָּפְקַדְנָה
3	mas.	יַפְקִידוּ	3	mas.	יָפְקְדוּ
	fem.	תַּפְקֵדְנָה		fem.	תָּפְקַדְנָה

CONJUGATIONS

TRANSITIVE

SING.	2	mas. fem.	הַפְקֵד הַפְקִידִי	SING.	2	mas. ...... fem. ......
PLU.	2	mas. fem.	הַפְקִידוּ הַפְקֵדְנָה	PLU.	2	mas. ...... fem. ......

} wanting

PAST

SINGULAR	1	mas. fem.	הִפְקַדְתִּי	SINGULAR	1	mas. fem.	הָפְקַדְתִּי
	2	mas. fem.	הִפְקַדְתָּ הִפְקַדְתְּ		2	mas. fem.	הָפְקַדְתָּ הָפְקַדְתְּ
	3	mas. fem.	הִפְקִיד הִפְקִידָה		3	mas. fem.	הָפְקַד הָפְקְדָה
PLURAL	1	mas. fem.	הִפְקַדְנוּ	PLURAL	1	mas. fem.	הָפְקַדְנוּ
	2	mas. fem.	הִפְקַדְתֶּם הִפְקַדְתֶּן		2	mas. fem.	הָפְקַדְתֶּם הָפְקַדְתֶּן
	3	mas. fem.	הִפְקִידוּ		3	mas. fem.	הָפְקְדוּ

REFLEXIVE FORM

ACTIVE MOVEMENT	PASSIVE MOVEMENT

FACULTATIVE

CONTIN. { mas. מִתְפַּקֵּד
         { fem. מִתְפַּקְּדָה

FINISH. { mas. ..... } wanting
        { fem. ..... }

NOMINAL VERB

absol. } הִתְפַּקֵּד
constr. }

TEMPORAL VERB

FUTURE

SINGULAR
1 { mas. } אֶתְפַּקֵּד
  { fem. }
2 { mas. תִּתְפַּקֵּד
  { fem. תִּתְפַּקְּדִי
3 { mas. יִתְפַּקֵּד
  { fem. תִּתְפַּקֵּד

PLURAL
1 { mas. } נִתְפַּקֵּד
  { fem. }
2 { mas. תִּתְפַּקְּדוּ
  { fem. תִּתְפַּקֵּדְנָה
3 { mas. יִתְפַּקְּדוּ
  { fem. תִּתְפַּקֵּדְנָה

CONJUGATIONS

TRANSITIVE

SING. 2	mas.	הִתְפַּקֵד
	fem.	הִתְפַּקְדִי
PLU. 2	mas.	הִתְפַּקְדוּ
	fem.	הִתְפַּקֵדְנָה

PAST

SINGULAR	1	mas. / fem.	הִתְפַּקַדְתִּי
	2	mas.	הִתְפַּקַדְתָּ
		fem.	הִתְפַּקַדְתְּ
	3	mas.	הִתְפַּקֵד
		fem.	הִתְפַּקְדָה
PLURAL	1	mas. / fem.	הִתְפַּקַדְנוּ
	2	mas.	הִתְפַּקַדְתֶּם
		fem.	הִתְפַּקַדְתֶּן
	3	mas. / fem.	הִתְפַּקְדוּ

Remarks upon the Derivative Conjugation.

I have not judged it necessary to change the typical verb which the Hebraists give as theme for this conjugation, because this verb lends itself to the four forms. I am going to present only its etymological meaning.

The primitive root פּוּק from which it is derived, contains the general idea of an alternating movement from one place to another, such as one would see, for example, in a pendulum. This idea coming out more distinctly in the verbalized root, signifies *to pass from one place to another, to be carried here and there, to go and come.* Here is clearly observed the opposed action of the two signs פּ and ק, of which the one opens the centre and the other cuts and designs the circumference. This root is joined, in order to compose the word of which we are speaking, to the root אד or יד, no less expressive, which, relating properly to the forefinger of the hand, signifies figuratively any object distinct or alone; an extract from abundance born of division: for this abundance is expressed in Hebrew by the same root considered under the contrary relation די.

Thus these two roots contracted in the compound פָּקַד, develop the idea of a movement which is carried alternately from one object to another: it is an *examination,* an *exploration,* an *inspection,* a *visit,* a *census,* etc; from this results the facultative פָּקֹד, *to be inspecting, examining, visiting;* and the nominal verb פָּקוֹד, *to visit, to examine, to inspect,* etc.

Positive Form.

Active movement. It must be remembered that the Chaldaic punctuation, following all the inflection of the vulgar pronunciation, corrupts very often the etymology. Thus it suppresses the verbal sign ו of the continued facultative, and substitutes either the *holem* or the *kamez* as in כֹּפֶר *appeasing, expiating;* אָבֵל *grieving, mourning, sorrowing.*

Sometimes one finds this same facultative terminated by the character י, to form a kind of qualificative, as in אֲסָרִי, *linking, enchaining, subjugating.*

I shall speak no further of the feminine changing the final character ה to ת, because it is a general rule.

The nominal assumes quite voluntarily the emphatic article ה, particularly when it becomes construct; then the Chaldaic punctuation again suppresses the verbal sign ו, as in לְמָשְׁחָה, *to annoint, according to the action of annointing, to coat over, to oil, to paint,* etc. I must state here, that this emphatic article can be added to nearly all the verbal modifications, but chiefly to both facultatives, to the nominal and the transitive. It can be found even in the future and the past, as one sees it in אֶשְׁמְרָה, *I shall guard;* בִּגַּדְתָּה, *he lied.*

When the nominal verb begins with the mother vowel א, this vowel blends with the affix of the first person future, disappears sometimes in the second, and has in the third, the point *holem;* thus אָסוֹף *to gather,* makes אֹסֶף *I shall gather;* תֵּאָסֵף or תֹּסֵף *thou shalt gather;* יֶאֱסֹף, *he shall gather:* thus, אָכוֹל *to feed oneself,* makes אֹכַל *I shall feed myself;* thus אָמוֹר *to say,* makes אֹמַר *I shall say;* תֹּאמַר, *thou shalt say;* יֹאמַר, *he shall say;* etc. Some Hebraists have made of this slight anomaly an irregular conjugation that they call *Quiescent Pe 'Aleph.*

These same Hebraists ready to multiply the difficulties, have also made an irregular conjugation of the verbs whose final character נ or ת, is not doubled in receiving the future ending נָה, or the affixes of the past תִּי, תָּ, תְּ, תֶּן, תֶּם, נוּ; but is blended with the ending of the affix, being supplied with the interior point: as one remarks it in כָּרוֹת

to suppress, which makes כָּרַתִּי, *I suppressed,* כָּרַתָּ *thou suppressed;* etc., or in שְׁכוֹן, *to inhabit,* which makes תִּשְׁכֹּנָּה, *you shall inhabit* (fem); *they shall inhabit;* שְׁכֹנָה, *inhabit* (fem.); שָׁכַנּוּ, *we shall inhabit;* etc. There is nothing perplexing in this. The only real difficulty results from the change of the character נ into ת, in the verb נָתוֹן, *to give,* which makes נָתַתִּי, *I gave,* נָתַתָּ, *thou gavest;* etc., I have already spoken of this anomaly in treating of the radical conjugation.

There exists a more considerable irregularity when the verb terminates with א or ה, and concerning which it is necessary to speak more fully. But as this anomaly is seen in the three conjugations I shall await the end of this chapter to take up the subject.

Passive Movement. The Chaldaic punctuation sometimes substitutes the *zere* for the *hirek* in the passive nominal, as can be seen in הֵאָסֵף *the action of being gathered;* or in הֵאָכֹל, *the action of being consummated.* One observes in this last example the appearance even of the *holem*. It is useless to dwell upon a thing which follows step by step the vulgar pronunciation and which yields to all its caprices. The characteristic sign and the mother vowel, these, are what should be examined with attention. One ought to be concerned with the point, only when there is no other means of discovering the meaning of a word.

Moreover, it is necessary to remark that the passive movement can become reciprocal and even superactive when the verb is not used in the active movement. Thus one finds נִשְׁמַר *he took care of himself;* נִשְׁבַּע *he swore; he bore witness,* etc.

Intensive Form.

Ever since the Chaldaic punctuation has, as I have said, suppressed the mother vowels י and ו, which are placed after the first verbal character, the one in the active movement and the other in the passive, there remains, in order to recognize this interesting form, whose force supplies the adverbial relation very rare in Hebrew, only the interior point of the second character. Therefore the utmost attention must be given.

All derivative verbs of two roots uncontracted as כִּלְכֵּל, *to achieve wholly*, כִּרְכֵּר, *to rise rapidly in the air*, etc.; in short, all verbs that the Hebraists name quadriliteral, because they are, in effect, composed of four letters in the nominal without including the verbal sign ו, belong to this form and follow it in its modifications.

Sometimes the point *hirek* which accompanies the first character of the verb in the intensive past, is replaced by the *zere* as in בֵּרֵךְ *he blessed fervently*.

The intensive form takes place in the active movement with as much method as without; sometimes it gives a contrary meaning to the positive verb: thus הָטוֹא *the action of sinning*, makes חָטָא *he sinned;* and הֻטָּא *he is purged from sin;* thus שָׁרוֹשׁ, *the action of taking root*, makes שָׁרַשׁ, *it took root;* and שֹׁרֵשׁ, *it was rooted up;* etc. The passive movement follows nearly the same modifications.

Excitative Form.

I have spoken sufficiently of the utility and usage of this form. It is characterized clearly enough to be readily recognized. One knows that its principal purpose is to transport the verbal action into another subject which it is a question of making act; however, it must be noticed that when the positive form does not exist, which sometimes happens, then it becomes simply declarative, according to the active or passive movement, with or without method. It is thus that one finds הִצְדִּיק, *he was declared just, he was justified:* הִרְשִׁיעַ *he was declared impious;* הֵקִיץ, *he awakened, he was aroused, he made re-*

pose cease; הִשְׁלִיךְ, *he projected;* הָשְׁלַךְ **he was projected;** etc.

Reflexive Form.

Besides this form being reciprocal at the same time as reflexive, that is to say, that the nominal הִתְפַּקֵּד, can signify alike, *to visit oneself, to visit each other,* or *to be aroused to visit;* it can also, according to circumstances, become simulatory, frequentative and even intensive, returning thus to its proper source; for, as I have said, this form is no other than the intensive, to which was added the characteristic syllable הת. One finds under these different acceptations: הִתְהַלֵּךְ, *he went about, he walked up and down, he went without stopping;* הִתְפַּלֵּל, *he offered himself to administer justice, to be magistrate;* etc.

I have spoken of the syncope and metathesis which substitute the syllable הת, for the article of the radical conjugation. Its repetition is unnecessary. It is also unnecessary for me to repeat that the emphatic article ה is placed indifferently for all the verbal modifications, and that the Chaldaic punctuation varies.

CONJUGATIONS

§. III.

Compound Radical Conjugation with the Initial Adjunction וֹ

POSITIVE FORM

ACTIVE MOVEMENT		PASSIVE MOVEMENT	

FACULTATIVE

	CONTINUED		CONTINUED
mas.	יוֹשֵׁב	mas.	נוֹשָׁב
fem.	יוֹשְׁבָה	fem.	נוֹשָׁבָה

FINISHED

mas.	יָשׁוֹב	
fem.	יָשׁוּבָה	

NOMINAL VERB

absol.	יָשׁוֹב	absol.	⎫	
constr.	שֶׁבֶת	constr.	⎬	הוּשָׁב

TEMPORAL VERB

FUTURE

SINGULAR
- 1 { m. / f. }   אֵשֵׁב
- 2 { m. }   תֵּשֵׁב
-    { f. }   תֵּשְׁבִי
- 3 { m. }   יֵשֵׁב
-    { f. }   תֵּשֵׁב

SINGULAR
- 1 { m. / f. }   אוּשַׁב
- 2 { m. }   תּוּשַׁב
-    { f. }   תּוּשְׁבִי
- 3 { m. }   יוּשַׁב
-    { f. }   תּוּשַׁב

225

226 THE HEBRAIC TONGUE RESTORED

FUTURE

PLURAL	1	m. / f.	נוֹשֵׁב	PLURAL	1	m. / f.	נוֹשֵׁב
	2	m.	תּוֹשְׁבוּ		2	m.	תּוֹשְׁבוּ
		f.	תּוֹשַׁבְנָה			f.	תּוֹשַׁבְנָה
	3	m.	יוֹשְׁבוּ		3	m.	יוֹשְׁבוּ
		f.	תּוֹשַׁבְנָה			f.	תּוֹשַׁבְנָה

(left column future: נֵשֵׁב, תֵּשְׁבוּ, תֵּשַׁבְנָה, יֵשְׁבוּ, תֵּשַׁבְנָה)

TRANSITIVE

SING.	2	mas.	שֵׁב	SING.	2	mas.	הוֹשֵׁב
		fem.	שְׁבִי			fem.	הוֹשְׁבִי
PLU.	2	mas.	שְׁבוּ	PLU.	2	mas.	הוֹשְׁבוּ
		fem.	שְׁבְנָה			fem.	הוֹשַׁבְנָה

PAST

SINGULAR	1	m. / f.	יָשַׁבְתִּי	SINGULAR	1	m. / f.	נוֹשַׁבְתִּ
	2	m.	יָשַׁבְתָּ		2	m.	נוֹשַׁבְתָּ
		f.	יָשַׁבְתְּ			f.	נוֹשַׁבְתְּ
	3	m.	יָשַׁב		3	m.	נוֹשַׁב
		f.	יָשְׁבָה			f.	נוֹשְׁבָה
PLURAL	1	m. / f.	יָשַׁבְנוּ	PLURAL	1	m. / f.	נוֹשַׁבְנוּ
	2	m.	יְשַׁבְתֶּם		2	m.	נוֹשַׁבְתֶּם
		f.	יְשַׁבְתֶּן			f.	נוֹשַׁבְתֶּן
	3	m.	יָשְׁבוּ		3	m.	נוֹשְׁבוּ
		f.				f.	

CONJUGATIONS

INTENSIVE FORM

ACTIVE MOVEMENT	PASSIVE MOVEMENT

FACULTATIVE

CONTINUED		CONTINUED	
mas.	מְיַשֵּׁב	*mas.*	מְיֻשָּׁב
fem.	מְיַשְּׁבָה	*fem.*	מְיֻשָּׁבָה

FINISHED

mas. ...... } wanting
fem. ...... }

NOMINAL VERB

| *absol.* } | יַשֵּׁב | *absol.* } | יֻשַּׁב |
| *constr.* } | | *constr.* } | |

TEMPORAL VERB

FUTURE

| *mas.* } | אֲיַשֵּׁב | *mas.* } | אֲיֻשַּׁב |
| *fem.* } | | *fem.* } | |

TRANSITIVE

| *mas.* } | יַשֵּׁב | *mas.* } | } wanting |
| *fem.* } | יַשְּׁבִי | *fem.* } | |

PAST

| *mas.* } | יִשַּׁבְתִּי | *mas.* } | יֻשַּׁבְתִּי |
| *fem.* } | | *fem.* } | |

EXCITATIVE FORM

FACULTATIVE

	CONTINUED			CONTINUED	
mas.	מוֹשִׁיב		*mas.*	מוּשָׁב	
fem.	מוֹשִׁיבָה		*fem.*	מוּשָׁבָה	

FINISHED

mas. ..... ⎫
fem. ..... ⎭ like the passive

NOMINAL VERB

| *absol.* | הוֹשִׁיב | *absol.* | ⎫ | הוּשַׁב |
| *constr.* | הוֹשֵׁב | *constr.* | ⎭ | |

TEMPORAL VERB

FUTURE

| *mas.* | ⎫ | אוֹשִׁיב | *mas.* | ⎫ | אוּשַׁב |
| *fem.* | ⎭ | | *fem.* | ⎭ | |

TRANSITIVE

| *mas.* | הוֹשֵׁב | *mas.* ..... | ⎫ | wanting |
| *fem.* | הוֹשִׁיבִי | *fem.* ..... | ⎭ | |

PAST

| *mas.* | ⎫ | הוֹשַׁבְתִּי | *mas.* | ⎫ | הוּשַׁבְתִּי |
| *fem.* | ⎭ | | *fem.* | ⎭ | |

CONJUGATIONS

Reflexive Form

ACTIVE AND PASSIVE MOVEMENT UNITED

FACULTATIVE

CONTIN. { mas. מִתְיַשֵּׁב
         { fem. מִתְיַשְּׁבָה

FINISH. { mas. .... } wanting
        { fem. .... }

NOMINAL VERB

absol. } הִתְיַשֵּׁב
constr. }

TEMPORAL VERB

FUTURE

mas. } אֶתְיַשֵּׁב
fem. }

TRANSITIVE

mas.   הִתְיַשֵּׁב
fem.   הִתְיַשְּׁבִי

PAST

mas. } הִתְיַשַּׁבְתִּי
fem. }

REMARKS ON THE COMPOUND RADICAL CONJUGATION.

Initial Adjunction י

The verb presented here as model is יָשׁוּב. I am about to proceed with its analysis. The root שׁוּב contains the idea of a return to a place, to a time, to a condition or an action, from which one had departed. It is the sign of the relative movement שׁ, which is united to that of interior, central and generative action ב. This return, being determined and manifested by the initial adjunction י, becomes a real sojourn, a taking possession of, an occupation, a habitation. Thus the compound radical verb יָשׁוּב can signify, according to circumstances, the action *of dwelling, of inhabiting, of sojourning, of taking possession;* etc.

Positive Form.

Active Movement. The initial adjunction י remains constant in the two facultatives, in the absolute nominal as well as in the past tense; but it disappears in the construct nominal, in the transitive and in the future. It seems indeed, that in this case the mother vowel י ought to be placed between the first and second character of the verbal root, and that one should say יְשִׁבֶת, *the action of occupying;* אֶשִׁיב, *I shall occupy;* שִׁיב, *occupy;* etc. But the Chaldaic punctuation having prevailed, has supplied it with the *segol* or the *zere*.

The simplicity of the transitive tense in this conjugation has made many savants, and notably Court de Gébelin, think that it should be regarded as the first of the verbal tenses. Already Leibnitz who felt keenly the need of etymological researches, had seen that in reality the transitive is, in the Teutonic idioms, the simplest of the tenses. President Desbrosses had spoken loudly in favour of this opinion, and abbé Bergier limited the whole compass of

Hebraic verbs to it. This opinion, which is not in the least to be held in contempt, finds support in what Du Halde said pertaining to the tongue of the Manchu Tartars whose verbs appear to originate from the transitive. But it is evident through the examination of the radical conjugation, that the nominal and the transitive of the verb, are *au fond* the same thing in Hebrew, and that the latter differs not from the former except by a modification purely mental. The Hebrews said קוֹם *the action of establishing* and קֹם *establish*. The purpose of the speaker, the accent which accompanied it could alone feel the difference. The nominal יְשׁוֹב differs here from the transitive שֵׁב, only because the initial adjunction י is unable to resist the influence of the modification. In the verbs where this mother vowel is not a simple adjunction but a sign, the transitive does not differ from the nominal. One finds, for example, יָרוֹשׁ *possess,* and יְרוֹשׁ, *the action of possessing.*

Verbs similiar to the one just cited, where the sign is not an adjunction, belong to the derivative conjugation. It is only a matter of a good dictionary to distinguish them carefully. A grammar suffices to declare their existence.

Passive movement. The initial adjunctiton י, being replaced in this movement by the mother vowel וֹ, varies no further, and gives to this conjugation all the strength of the derivative conjugation.

Intensive Form.

This form is little used in this conjugation, for the reason that the positive form itself is only a sort of intensity given to the radical verb by means of the initial adjunction י. When by chance, it is found employed, one sees that this adjunction has taken all the force of a sign and remains with the verb to which it is united

Excitative Form.

The initial adjunction ׳, is replaced in the active movement by the intellectual sign ו, and in the passive movement by the convertible sign ו. This change made, the compound radical verb varies no more, and follows the course of the derivative verbs as it has followed it in the preceding form. If it sometimes happens that this change is not affected as in הֵיטִיב *to do good*, the verb remains none the less indivisible. This changes nothing in its conjugation.

Reflexive Form.

The compound radical verb continues under this new form to demonstrate all the strength of a derivative verb. The only remark, somewhat important, that I have to make, is relative to the three verbs following, which replace their initial adjunction ׳, by the convertible sign ו, become consonant.

יָדֹוע	to understand	הִתְוָדֵע	to be understood
יָכֹוח	to prove, to argue	הִתְוָכֵח	to be proven
יָסֹור	to correct, to instruct	הִתְוָסֵר	to be corrected

CONJUGATIONS

§ IV.

Compound Radical Conjugation.
with the Initial Adjunction נ

Positive Form

	ACTIVE MOVEMENT		PASSIVE MOVEMENT

FACULTATIVE

	CONTINUED		CONTINUED
mas.	נוֹגֵשׁ	mas.	נִגָּשׁ
fem.	נוֹגְשָׁה	fem.	נִגָּשָׁה

FINISHED

mas.	נָגוּשׁ	fem.	נְגוּשָׁה

NOMINAL VERB

absol.	נָגוֹשׁ	absol.	} הִנָּגֵשׁ
constr.	גֶּשֶׁת	constr.	}

TEMPORAL VERB
FUTURE

SINGULAR
1 {m./f.} אֶנָּגֵשׁ
2 {m.} תִּנָּגֵשׁ
2 {f.} תִּנָּגְשִׁי
3 {m.} יִנָּגֵשׁ
3 {f.} תִּנָּגֵשׁ

SINGULAR
1 {m./f.} אֶנָּגֵשׁ
2 {m.} תִּנָּגֵשׁ
2 {f.} תִּנָּגְשִׁי
3 {m.} יִנָּגֵשׁ
3 {f.} תִּנָּגֵשׁ

PLURAL
1 {m./f.} נִנָּגֵשׁ
2 {m.} תִּנָּגְשׁוּ
2 {f.} תִּנָּגַשְׁנָה
3 {m.} יִנָּגְשׁוּ
3 {f.} תִּנָּגַשְׁנָה

PLURAL
1 {m./f.} נִנָּגֵשׁ
2 {m.} תִּנָּגְשׁוּ
2 {f.} תִּנָּגַשְׁנָה
3 {m.} יִנָּגְשׁוּ
3 {f.} תִּנָּגַשְׁנָה

TRANSITIVE

SING. 2	m.	נְגֵשׁ	SING. 2	m.	הִנָּגֵשׁ
	f.	גְּשִׁי		f.	הִנָּגְשִׁי
PLU. 2	m.	גְּשׁוּ	PLU. 2	m.	הִנָּגְשׁוּ
	f.	גְּשְׁנָה		f.	הִנָּגֵשְׁנָה

PAST

SINGULAR 1	m. / f.	נָגַשְׁתִּי	SINGULAR 1	m. / f.	נִגַּשְׁתִּי
2	m.	נָגַשְׁתָּ	2	m.	נִגַּשְׁתָּ
	f.	נָגַשְׁתְּ		f.	נִגַּשְׁתְּ
3	m.	נָגַשׁ	3	m.	נִגַּשׁ
	f.	נָגְשָׁה		f.	נִגְּשָׁה
PLURAL 1	m. / f.	נָגַשְׁנוּ	PLURAL 1	m. / f.	נִגַּשְׁנוּ
2	m.	נָגַשְׁתֶּם	2	m.	נִגַּשְׁתֶּם
	f.	נָגַשְׁתֶּן		f.	נִגַּשְׁתֶּן
3	m. / f.	נָגְשׁוּ	3	m. / f.	נִגְּשׁוּ

CONJUGATIONS   235

Intensive Form

ACTIVE MOVEMENT   PASSIVE MOVEMENT

FACULTATIVE

CONTINUED

mas.	מְנַגֵּשׁ	*mas.*	מְנֻגָּשׁ
fem.	מְנַגְּשָׁה	*fem.*	מְנֻגָּשָׁה

FINISHED

mas. .... ⎫
fem. .... ⎬ like the passive

NOMINAL VERB.

absol. ⎫ נַגֵּשׁ   *absol.* ⎫ נֻגּוֹשׁ
constr. ⎭   *constr.* ⎭

TEMPORAL VERB

FUTURE

mas. ⎫ אֲנַגֵּשׁ   *mas.* ⎫ אֲנֻגַּשׁ
fem. ⎭   *fem.* ⎭

TRANSITIVE

mas. ⎫ נַגְּשִׁי   *mas.* .... ⎫ wanting
fem. ⎭   *fem.* .... ⎭

PAST

mas. ⎫ נִגַּשְׁתִּי   *mas.* ⎫ נֻגַּשְׁתִּי
fem. ⎭   *fem.* ⎭

EXCITATIVE FORM

| ACTIVE MOVEMENT | PASSIVE MOVEMENT |

FACULTATIVE

CONTINUED

	ACTIVE		PASSIVE
mas.	מַגִּישׁ	mas.	מֻגָּשׁ
fem.	מַגִּישָׁה	fem.	מֻגָּשָׁה

FINISHED

mas. .... ⎫
fem. .... ⎬ like the passive

NOMINAL VERB

	ACTIVE		PASSIVE
absol.	הַגִּישׁ	absol. ⎫	הֻגֵּשׁ
constr.	הַגֵּשׁ	constr. ⎬	

TEMPORAL VERB

FUTURE

| mas. ⎫ | אַגִּישׁ | mas. ⎫ | אֻגַּשׁ |
| fem. ⎭ | | fem. ⎭ | |

TRANSITIVE

| mas. ⎫ | הִגַּשְׁתִּי | mas. ⎫ | הֻגַּשְׁתִּי |
| fem. ⎭ | | fem. ⎭ | |

PAST

| mas. | הִגֵּשׁ | mas. ⎫ | wanting |
| fem. | הִגִּישִׁי | fem. .... ⎭ | |

CONJUGATIONS

REFLEXIVE FORM

ACTIVE MOVEMENT   PASSIVE MOVEMENT

FACULTATIVE

CONTIN. { *mas.* מִתְנַגֵּשׁ
{ *fem.* מִתְנַגְּשָׁה

FINISH. { *mas.* ⎫
{ *fem.* ..... ⎬ wanting

NOMINAL VERB

absol. ⎫
constr. ⎬ הִתְנַגֵּשׁ

TEMPORAL VERB

FUTURE

mas. ⎫
fem. ⎬ אֶתְנַגֵּשׁ

TRANSITIVE

mas. הִתְנַגֵּשׁ

fem. הִתְנַגְּשִׁי

PAST

mas. ⎫
fem. ⎬ הִתְנַגַּשְׁתִּי

REMARKS ON THE COMPOUND RADICAL CONJUGATION.

INITIAL ADJUNCTION נ.

Here is the somewhat difficult etymology of the verb נָגַשׁ, which I give as type, thus following the usage of the Hebraists, from which I never digress without the strongest reasons.

The root גֻ or גֹה, offers the general idea of some sort of detachment, destined to contain something in itself, as a sheath; or to pass through, as a channel. This root united to the sign of relative movement, offers in the word גֻשׁ, the most restrained idea of a local detachment, of a letting go. This detachment being arrested and brought back upon itself by the initial adjunction נ, will signify an approaching, a nearness; and the compound radical verb נָגַשׁ, will express the action of drawing near, of joining, of meeting, of approaching, etc.

POSITIVE FORM.

Active movement. The initial adjunction נ, disappears in the construct nominal, in the future and transitive, as I have already remarked concerning the initial adjunction י; it remains the same in the two facultatives, in the absolute nominal and in the past. I infer that in the original tongue of Moses and before the Chaldaic punctuation had been adopted, it was the sign ו which was placed between the first and second character of the verbal root, and which read נְגוֹשַׁת, *the action of approaching,* אֶגּוֹשׁ *I shall approach,* גּוּשׁ *approach.* This mother vowel has been replaced by the point *patah*. A thing which makes this inference very believable, is that one still finds it in several verbs belonging to this conjugation, which preserve this sign in the future, such as יָכֹול *he shall fail,* etc.

It must be observed that in the verb נָקוֹה, *to take, to draw to oneself*, the nominal sometimes takes the character ל in place of the initial adjunction נ, and follows the course of the compound radical conjugation, of which I have given the example; so that one finds very often לְקֹחַ, or קַחַת *the action of taking*, אֶקַּח *I shall take*, קַח *take*, etc.

Passive movement. The Chaldaic punctuation having suppressed the mother vowel, which should characterize this movement, has made it very difficult to distinguish the active movement, especially in the past. It can only be distinguished in this tense by the meaning of the phrase.

INTENSIVE FORM.

This form is but little used. When it is however, it should be observed that the initial adjunction נ, takes the force of a sign and is no longer separated from its verb. It acts in the same manner as the initial adjunction י, of which I have spoken. The compound radical conjugation therefore, does not differ from the derivative conjugation.

EXCITATIVE FORM.

This form is remarkable in both movements, because the adjunctive character נ, disappears wholly and is only supplied by the interior point placed in the first character of the root. It is obvious that in the origin of the Hebraic tongue, the compound radical conjugation differed here from the radical conjugation, only by the interior point of which I have spoken, and that the mother vowel י, was placed between the two radical characters in the active movement; whereas the convertible sign ו, was shown in front of the first radical character in the passive movement. One should say אַגִּישׁ, *I shall make approach;* as one finds הַגִּישׁ *to make approach*, אֻגַּשׁ *I shall be excited to approach;* as one finds הוּגַשׁ, *the action of being excited to approach;* but almost invariably the Chaldaic punctuation has replaced these mother vowels by the *hirek* or the *zere,* in the active movement, and by the *kibbuz* in the passive movement.

Reflexive Form

The initial adjunction נ, never being separated from the root, reappearing in this form, gives it the character of a derivative verb.

CONJUGATIONS

§ V.

Compound Radical Conjugation with the Terminative Adjunction

Positive Form

ACTIVE MOVEMENT	PASSIVE MOVEMENT

FACULTATIVE

CONTINUED	CONTINUED
סוֹבֵב	נָסָב
סוֹבְבָה	נְסַבָה

FINISHED

mas.	סָבוּב	fem.	סְבוּבָה

NOMINAL VERB

| absol. | סוֹב | absol. | הִסּוֹב |
| constr. | סְבוֹב | constr. | |

TEMPORAL VERB

FUTURE

SINGULAR	1 { m. / f. }	אָסוֹב	SINGULAR	1 { m. / f. }	אֶסַּב
	2 { m.	תָּסוֹב		2 { m.	תִּסַּב
	f.	תָּסוֹבִי		f.	תִּסַּבִּי
	3 { m.	יָסוֹב		3 { m.	יָסַּב
	f.	תָּסוֹב		f.	תִּסַּב

TEMPORAL VERB. FUTURE

PLURAL	1 {m./f.}	נָסוֹב	PLURAL	1 {m./f.}	נָסֹב
	2 {m.}	תְּסוֹבּוּ		2 {m.}	תִּסֹבּוּ
	{f.}	תְּסֻבֶּינָה		{f.}	תְּסֻבֶּינָה
	3 {m.}	יָסֹבּוּ		3 {m.}	יָסֹבּוּ
	{f.}	תְּסֻבֶּינָה		{f.}	תְּסֻבֶּינָה

TRANSITIVE

SING.	2 {mas.}	סוֹב	SING.	2 {mas.}	הָסֵב
	{fem.}	סוֹבִי		{fem.}	הָסֵבִי
PLU.	2 {mas.}	סֹבּוּ	PLU.	2 {mas.}	הָסֵבּוּ
	{fem.}	סֻבֶּינָה		{fem.}	הַסֻבֶּינָה

PAST

SINGULAR	1 {m./f.}	סַבּוֹתִי	SINGULAR	1 {m./f.}	נְסַבּוֹתִי
	2 {m.}	סַבּוֹתָ		2 {m.}	נְסַבּוֹתָ
	{f.}	סַבּוֹת		{f.}	נְסַבּוֹת
	3 {m.}	סַב		3 {m.}	נָסַב
	{f.}	סַבָּה		{f.}	נָסַבָּה
PLURAL	1 {m./f.}	סַבּוֹנָה	PLURAL	1 {m./f.}	נְסַבּוֹנָה
	2 {m.}	סַבּוֹתֶם		2 {m.}	נְסַבּוֹתֶם
	{f.}	סַבּוֹתֶן		{f.}	נְסַבּוֹתֶן
	3 {m./f.}	סַבּוּ		3 {m./f.}	נָסַבּוּ

CONJUGATIONS

INTENSIVE FORM

ACTIVE MOVEMENT	PASSIVE MOVEMENT

FACULTATIVE

CONTINUED / CONTINUED

| *mas.* | מְסוֹבֵב | *mas.* | מְסוֹבָב |
| *fem.* | מְסוֹבְבָה | *fem.* | מְסוֹבָבָה |

FINISHED

mas. .....
fem. ..... } like the passive

NOMINAL VERB

absol. }
constr. } סוֹבֵב   *absol.* }
                          constr. } סוֹבָב

TEMPORAL VERB

FINISHED

mas. }
fem. } אֲסוֹבֵב   *mas.* }
                          fem. } אֲסוֹבָב

TRANSITIVE

| *mas.* | סוֹבֵב | *mas.* ..... |
| *fem.* | סוֹבְבִי | *fem.* ..... } wanting |

PAST

mas. }
fem. } סוֹבַבְתִּי   *mas.* }
                          fem. } סוֹבַבְתִּי

EXCITATIVE FORM

| ACTIVE MOVEMENT | | PASSIVE MOVEMENT | |

FACULTATIVE

CONTINUED

mas.	מֵסֵב	*mas.*	מוּסָב
fem.	מְסִבָּה	*fem.*	מוּסָבָה

FINISHED

mas. ......⎱
fem. ......⎰ like the passive

NOMINAL VERB

| *absol.* ⎱ | הָסֵב | *absol.* ⎱ | הוּסָב |
| *constr.* ⎰ | | *constr.* ⎰ | |

TEMPORAL VERB

FUTURE

| *mas.* ⎱ | אָסֵב | *mas.* ⎱ | אוּסָב |
| *fem.* ⎰ | | *fem.* ⎰ | |

TRANSITIVE

| *mas.* | הָסֵב | *mas.* ......⎱ | wanting |
| *fem.* | וְהָסְבִי | *fem.* ......⎰ | |

PAST

| *mas.* ⎱ | הֲסִבּוֹתִי | *mas.* ⎱ | הוּסְבּוֹתִי |
| *fem.* ⎰ | | *fem.* ⎰ | |

CONJUGATIONS

Reflexive Form

ACTIVE AND PASSIVE MOVEMENT UNITED

FACULTATIVE

CONTIN. { mas. מִסְתּוֹבֵב
{ fem. מִסְתּוֹבְבָה

FINISH. { mas. .....
{ fem. ..... } wanting

NOMINAL VERB

absol. }
constr. } הִסְתּוֹבֵב

TEMPORAL VERB

FUTURE

mas. }
fem. } אֶסְתּוֹבֵב

TRANSITIVE

mas. הִסְתּוֹבֵב

fem. הִסְתּוֹבְבִי

PAST

mas. }
fem. } הִסְתּוֹבַבְתִּי

REMARKS ON THE COMPOUND RADICAL CONJUGATION

TERMINATIVE ADJUNCTION

This conjugation is, in general, only a modification of the radical conjugation. It seems also that this may be the intensive form represented by the verb קוֹמֵם, for example, which has been given as positive form, so that the following forms may have greater energy.

The root סב, from which is derived the compound radical verb סוֹבֵב, which I give here as type following the Hebraists, being formed from the sign of interior and central action ב, and from the sign of circular movement ס expresses necessarily any kind of movement which operates around a centre. The duplication of the last character ב, in giving more force to the central point, tends to bring back the circumference ס, and consequently to intensify the action of turning, of closing in turning, of enveloping, of *surrounding* in fact, expressed by the verb in question.

POSITIVE FORM

Active movement. The final character ב, which has been doubled to form the compound radical verb סוֹבֵב, is only found in the two facultatives. It disappears in all the rest of the conjugation, which is, in substance, only the radical conjugation according to the intensive form, with a few slight differences brought about by the Chaldaic punctuation. The sole mark by which one can distinguish it, is the interior point placed in the second character of the verbal root, to indicate the prolonged accent which resulted no doubt from the double consonant.

Passive movement. This movement experiences a great variation in the vowel point. The facultatives and the nominals are often found marked by the *zere*, as in נְמֵס, *becoming dissolved, falling into dissolution;* הֵמַס

to be dissolved, liquified; הֵחָל *to be profaned, divulged;* etc. It is necessary in general, to be distrustful of the punctuation and to devote oneself to the meaning

Intensive Form

This form differs from the intensive radical only in this; that the Chaldaic punctuation has replaced almost uniformly the sign וֹ, by the point *holem*. Care must be taken, before giving it a signification, to examine well the final character which is doubled; for it is upon it alone that this signification depends.

Excitative Form

Again here the excitative radical form, (exception being made of the sign י,) is replaced in the active movement by the point *zere*. The passive movement is found a little more characterized by the mother vowel וֹ, which one finds added to the verbal root in some persons of the past.

Reflexive Form

The characteristic syllable הת, is simply added to the intensive form, as we have already remarked in the radical conjugation; but here it undergoes metathesis: that is to say, when placed before a verb which begins with the character ס, the ת must be transferred to follow this same character, in the same manner as one sees it in the nominal, where instead of reading הִתְסוֹבֵב one reads הִסְתוֹבֵב.

§ VI.

Irregularities in the Three Conjugations

I have already spoken of the trifling anomalies which are found in verbs beginning with the character א, or ending with the characters נ or ת.

Verbs of the three conjugations can be terminated

with the mother vowels א or ה, and in this case they undergo some variations in their course.

When it is the vowel א, which constitutes the final character of any verb whatever, as in the radical בוא *to come;* the compound ברוא, *to create;* the compound radical יצא, *to appear;* or נשׂא, *to raise;* this vowel becomes ordinarily mute as to pronunciation, and is not marked with the Chaldaic point. Nevertheless, as it remains in the different verbal forms, the irregularity which results from its lack of pronunciation is not perceptible, and should be no obstacle to the one who studies Hebrew only to understand and to translate it. The rabbis alone, who still cantillate this extinct tongue, make a particular conjugation of this irregularity.

There is no difficulty for us to know that the radical בוא, *the action of coming,* follows the radical conjugation,

אָבוֹא	I shall come	בָּאתִי	I came
תָּבוֹא	thou wilt come	בָּאתָ	thou camest
יָבוֹא	he will come	בָּא	he came
	etc.		*etc.*

or that the compound בְּרוֹא, or בָּראת, *the action of creating,* is conjugated in a like manner.

אֶבְרָא or אִבְרוֹא	I shall create	בָּרָאתִי	I created
תִּבְרָא	thou wilt create	בָּרָאתָ	thou createdst
יִבְרָא	he will create	בָּרָא	he created
	etc.		*etc.*

But when it is the vowel ה which constitutes the final character of the verb, then the difficulty becomes considerable, for this reason. This vowel not only remains mute, but disappears or is sometimes changed to another vowel; so that it would be impossible to recognize the verb, if one had not a model to which it might be related. Therefore I shall present here this model, taking for type the nominal גלוֹה or גלוֹת, and giving the etymological analysis.

This verb belongs to the root גּוּ, of which I spoke in the case of the compound radical verb נגוֹשׁ, and which contains the idea of some sort of detachment. This root, united to the sign of expansive movement ל, expresses as verb, the action of being released from a place, or from a veil, a vestment, a covering; the action of being shown uncovered, revealed, released; being set at liberty; etc.

It must be observed that the greater part of the verbs belonging to the three regular conjugations also receive modifications from what I call the irregular conjugation, according as they are terminated with the character ה, either as radical, derivative or compound radical verbs.

Nevertheless there are some verbs which terminate in this same character הּ, (marked with the interior point to distinguish it,) which are regular; that is to say, which follow the derivative conjugation to which they belong. These verbs are the four following:

נָבֹהַּ   the action of excelling, of surpassing, of exalting

כָּמֹהַּ   the action of languidly desiring, of languishing

נָגֹהַּ   the action of emitting, or of reflecting light

תָּמֹהַּ   the action of being astonished by its *éclat*, of being dazzled.

§ VI.
Irregular Conjugations
Positive Form

ACTIVE MOVEMENT		PASSIVE MOVEMENT	

FACULTATIVE
CONTINUED

mas.	גּוֹלֶה	*mas.*	נִגְלֶה
fem.	גּוֹלָה	*fem.*	נִגְלָה

FINISHED

mas.	גָלוּי
fem.	גְלוּיָה

NOMINAL VERB

absol.	גָלוֹה	*absol.*	הִגָּלוֹה
constr.	גְלוֹת	*constr.*	הִגָּלוֹת

TEMPORAL VERB
FUTURE

SINGULAR
1 m./f. אֶגְלֶה ⋯ אֶגָּלֶה
2 m. תִּגְלֶה ⋯ תִּגָּלֶה
2 f. תִּגְלִי ⋯ תִּגָּלִי
3 m. יִגְלֶה ⋯ יִגָּלֶה
3 f. תִּגְלֶה ⋯ תִּגָּלֶה

PLURAL
1 m./f. נִגְלֶה ⋯ נִגָּלֶה
2 m. תִּגְלוּ ⋯ תִּגָּלוּ
2 f. תִּגְלֶינָה ⋯ תִּגָּלֶינָה
3 m. יִגְלוּ ⋯ יִגָּלוּ
3 f. תִּגְלֶינָה ⋯ תִּגָּלֶינָה

CONJUGATIONS

TRANSITIVE

SING. 2	mas.	גְּלֵה	SING. 2	mas.	הַגְלֵה
	fem.	גְּלִי		fem.	הַגְלִי
PLU. 2	mas.	גְּלוּ		mas.	הַגְלוּ
	fem.	גְּלֶינָה		fem.	הַגְלֶינָה

PAST

SINGULAR 1	m. / f.	גָּלִיתִי	SINGULAR 1	m. / f.	נִגְלֵיתִי
2	m.	גָּלִיתָ	2	m.	נִגְלֵיתָ
	f.	גָּלִית		f.	נִגְלֵית
3	m.	גָּלָה	3	m.	נִגְלָה
	f.	גָּלְתָה		f.	נִגְלְתָה
PLURAL 1	m. / f.	גָּלִינוּ	PLURAL 1	m. / f.	נִגְלֵינוּ
2	m.	גְּלִיתֶם	2	m.	נִגְלֵיתֶם
	f.	גְּלִיתֶן		f.	נִגְלֵיתֶן
3	m. / f.	גָּלוּ	3	m. / f.	נִגְלוּ

INTENSIVE FORM

| ACTIVE MOVEMENT | PASSIVE MOVEMENT |

FACULTATIVE

CONTINUED

mas.	מְגַלֶּה	mas.	מְגֻלֶּה
fem.	מְגַלָּה	fem.	מְגֻלָּה

FINISHED

mas. .....}
fem. .....} like the passive

NOMINAL VERB

absol.	גַלֵּה	absol.	גֻלֹּה
constr.	גַלּוֹה	constr.	גֻלּוֹת

TEMPORAL VERB

FUTURE

mas.}
fem.} אֲגַלֶּה

mas.}
fem.} אֲגֻלֶּה

TRANSITIVE

mas.	גַלֵּה	mas.	}wanting
fem.	גַלִּי	fem.	

PAST

mas.}
fem.} גִּלִּיתִי

mas.}
fem.} גֻלֵּיתִי

CONJUGATIONS

Excitative Form

ACTIVE MOVEMENT   **PASSIVE MOVEMENT**

FACULTATIVE

CONTINUED

	ACTIVE		PASSIVE
mas.	מַגְלֶה	*mas.*	מֻגְלֶה
fem.	מַגְלָה	*fem.*	מֻגְלָה

FINISHED

mas. ......
fem. ...... } like the **passive**

NOMINAL VERB

	ACTIVE		PASSIVE
absol.	הַגְלֵה	*absol.*	הָגְלֵה
constr.	הַגְלוֹת	*constr.*	הָגְלוֹת

TEMPORAL VERB

FUTURE

	ACTIVE		PASSIVE
mas. }	אַגְלֶה	*mas.* }	אָגְלֶה
fem. }		*fem.* }	

TRANSITIVE

	ACTIVE		PASSIVE
mas.	הַגְלֵה	*mas.* ..... }	wanting
fem.	הַגְלִי	*fem.* ..... }	

PAST

	ACTIVE		PASSIVE
mas. }	הִגְלֵיתִי	*mas.* }	הָגְלֵיתִי
fem. }		*fem.* }	

253

Reflexive Form

ACTIVE AND PASSIVE MOVEMENT UNITED.

FACULTATIVE

CONTIN. { mas.   מִתְנַלֶּה
       { fem.   מִתְנַלָּה

FINISH. { mas. ………
      { fem. ……… } wanting.

NOMINAL VERB

absol. }
constr. } הִתְנַלּוֹת

TEMPORAL VERB

FUTURE

mas. }
fem. } אֶתְנַלֶּה

TRANSITIVE

mas. } הִתְנַלֶּה
fem. } הִתְנַלִי

PAST

mas. }
fem. } הִתְנַלִּיתִי

CHAPTER X.

CONSTRUCTION OF VERBS: ADVERBIAL RELATIONS: PARAGOGIC CHARACTERS: CONCLUSION

§ I.

UNION OF VERBS WITH VERBAL AFFIXES

I call the Construction of Verbs, their union with the verbal affixes. I have already shown the manner in which the nominal affixes are united to nouns. It remains for me to indicate here the laws which follow the verbal affixes when united to verbs.

These laws, if we omit the petty variations of the vowel points, can be reduced to this sole rule, namely; every time that any verbal modification whatsoever, receives an affix, it receives it by being constructed with it: that is to say, that if this modification, whatever it may be, has a construct, it employs it in this case.

Now let us glance rapidly over all the verbal modifications according to the rank that they occupy in the table of conjugations.

FACULTATIVES

The facultatives belong to nouns with which they form a distinct class. When they receive the verbal affix it is after the manner of nouns.

פּוֹקְדֵנִי	visiting me	(him)
פּוֹקְדַי	" "	(them, *m.*)
פּוֹקַדְתִּי	" "	(her)
פּוֹקְדוֹתַי	" "	(them, *f.*)
פּוֹקְדֵנוּ	" "	(him)
פּוֹקְדֵינוּ	" "	(them, *m.*)
פּוֹקַדְתְּנוּ	" "	(her)
פּוֹקְדוֹתֵינוּ	" "	(them, *f.*)

Those facultatives of the irregular conjugation which terminate in the character ה, lose it in the construct state.

עֹשֵׂנִי	making me (him)
רֹאִי or רֹאָנִי	seeing me (him)
מְלַמֶּדְךָ	teaching thee (him)
רֹדֵם	domineering them, *m.* (him)
רֹדֵן	" them, *f.* (him)
מְלַמְּדַי	teaching me (them)

NOMINAL VERB

I have already given the nominal verb united to the nominal and verbal affixes. I have been careful, in giving the table of the different conjugations, to indicate always the nominal construct, when this construct is distinguished from the absolute nominal. So that one might with a little attention recognize easily any verb whatsoever, by the nominal when it has the affix. Here are, besides, some examples to fix the ideas in this respect and to accustom the reader to the varieties of the punctuation.

קוּמִי or קָמִי	the action of establishing myself; my establishment
תֻּמִּי	the action of perfecting myself; my perfection
שׁוּבֵנִי	the action of restoring myself; my return, resurrection
פָּקְדִי	the action of visiting myself; of examining myself; my examination
הִפָּקְדוֹ	the action of being visited by another; his visit
פָּקְדֵנִי	the action of visiting myself, of inspecting myself diligently

הַפְקִידָהּ	the action of making her visit, of arousing her to visit
שִׁבְתּוֹ	the action of occupying, of inhabiting, of dwelling
לִרְתָּהּ	the action of bringing forth (*fem*)
גִּשְׁתְּךָ	the action of thy approaching (*mas*); thy approach
תִּתִּי	the action of giving myself

The emphatic article ה, when added to a nominal, is changed to ת, following the rules of the construct state.

אַהֲבָתוֹ	the action of loving him greatly
קׇרְבָתָם	the action of pressing them closely
מׇשְׁחָתִי	the action of consecrating me, of anointing me with holy oil

The irregular conjugation loses sometimes the character ה but more often changes it to ת.

TEMPORAL VERB

FUTURE

The sign ו which is in the greater part of the verbal modifications of the future, is lost in the construct state. The final character does not change in the three regular conjugations. I shall now present in its entirety, one of the persons of the future, united to the verbal affixes, taking my example from the derivative conjugation as the most used.

		Hebrew	Meaning
SINGULAR AFFIXES	mas.	יִפְקְדֵנִי	he will visit me
	fem.	יִפְקְדִי	
	mas.	יִפְקָדְךָ	he will visit thee
	fem.	יִפְקְדֵךְ	
	mas.	יִפְקְדוֹ or יִפְקְדֵנוּ	he will visit him
	fem.	יִפְקְדָהּ or יִפְקְדֶנָּה	he will visit her
PLURAL AFFIXES	mas.	יִפְקְדֵנוּ	he will visit us
	fem.		
	mas.	יִפְקָדְכֶם	he will visit you
	fem.	יִפְקָדְכֶן	
	mas.	יִפְקְדֵם	he will visit them
	fem.	יִפְקְדֵן	

It must be observed that the affix ו is changed quite frequently to הוּ, and usually one finds יִפְקְדֵהוּ instead of יִפְקְדֵנוּ or יִפְקְדוֹ.

In the irregular conjugation, the temporal modifications of the future which terminate in the character ה, lose this character in being constructed. Here are some examples, in which I have compared designedly these irregularities and some others of little importance.

CONSTRUCTION OF VERBS 259

יְסֻבֶּנּוּ	he will surround him
תְּסוֹבְכֵנִי	thou wilt surround me
תְּקִמֵנִי	thou wilt establish me
יִרְאַנִי	he will see me
יֶאֱהָבֵנִי	he will love me
יְשַׁבִּיעֵנִי	he will crown me with blessings
יַבְדִּילֵנִי	he will separate me with care
יְסֻבֵּנוּ	he will make us surrounded
יְבָרְכֶנְהוּ	he will bless him fervently
יִרְאָנוּ	he will see us
תִּרְאַנִי	she will see me
יְכֻנֵּנוּ	he will fashion us
יוֹשִׁיבֵנוּ	he will make me dwell
אֲבָרְכֵם	I will bless them

TRANSITIVE

The transitive modifications are very similar to those of the future: that is to say that the verbal sign וֹ disappears in the construct state. The final character remains mute.

פָּקְדֵנִי	visit me (*mas.*)	פָּקְדוּנוּ	visit us
פִּקְדִינִי	visit me (*fem.*)	שְׁאָלוּנוּ	ask us
שְׁמָעֵנִי	hear me	תְּנֵם	give them
שַׂמְּחֵנִי	gladden me well	דָּעֵן	know them
חָנֵּנִי	accord me grace	הֲקִימֵנוּ	make us established
נְחֵנִי	lead me	קַבְּצֵנוּ	gather us
קָבְנוּ	curse him	חָקְרֵם	consider them

Past

In the temporal modifications of the past, the first person singular and plural, the second and third person masculine singular, and the third person of the plural, change only the vowel point in being constructed with the affixes: but the second and third person of the feminine singular, and the second of the masculine and feminine plural, change the final character; as:

			absol.	constr.	
SINGULAR	1	mas. / fem.	פָּקַדְתִּי	פְּקַדְתִּי	I visited
	2	mas.	פָּקַדְתָּ	פְּקַדְתַּ	thou "
		fem.	פָּקַדְתְּ	פְּקַדְתִּי	
	3	mas.	פָּקַד	פְּקַד	he "
		fem.	פָּקְדָה	פְּקָדַת	she "
PLURAL	1	mas. / fem.	פָּקַדְנוּ	פְּקַדְנוּ	we "
	2	mas.	פְּקַדְתֶּם	פְּקַדְתּוּ	you "
		fem.	פְּקַדְתֶּן		
	3	mas. / fem.	פָּקְדוּ	פְּקָדוּ	they "

with affix

פְּקַדְתִּיךָ	I visited thee	פְּקָדַתּוֹ	she visited him
פְּקַדְתַּנִי / פְּקַדְתִּינִי	thou " me	פְּקָדָנוּם	we " them
		פְּקַדְתּוּנִי	you " us
פְּקָדָהּ	he " her	פְּקָדוּן	they " them

CONSTRUCTION OF VERBS

It is needless for me to dwell upon each of these modifications in particular. I shall conclude by giving some examples taken from different forms and from different conjugations.

פְקָדוֹ	he visited him diligently
אֲרָרָהּ	he cursed her violently
גִלְגַלְתִּיךָ	I encircled thee well
צִוִּיתִיךָ	I confirm thee much
הוֹרַדְתֵּנוּ	thou madest us descend
הֶעֱלִיתָנוּ	thou madest us rise
הֵפִיצָךְ	he made himself scattered
הוֹדְעָךְ	he made himself known
הַדְמָנוּ	he made us silent
הֱשִׁיבוּם	he made them return
שָׂמְךָ	he placed thee
שָׂמַתְהוּ	she placed him
שָׂמוּךְ	they were placed
קְרָאוֹ	he called him
עָשָׂהוּ	he made him
גִּלִּיתוֹ	thou revealedst him
יְכָלְתִּיו	I subdued him
מְצָאתָהּ	thou foundedst her
שׁוֹבַכְתָּךְ	she perverted thee
הֲזִיתִיךָ	I perceived thee

etc.

§ II.

ADVERBIAL RELATIONS

In Chapter IV of this Grammar, I have stated that the Relation ought to be considered under three connections, according to the part of speech with which it preserves the most analogy. I have called *designative relation*, that which appears to me to belong most expressly to the sign, and I have treated it under the name of *article*: I have then named *nominal relation*, that which has appeared to me to replace more especially the noun and to act in its absence, and I have called it *pronoun*: now this latter is what I qualify by the name of *adverbial relation*, because it seems to form a sort of bond between the noun and the verb, and without being either the one or the other, to participate equally in both. I shall treat of this last kind of relation under the name of *adverb*.

I beg my reader to remember that I do not confound the adverb with the modificative. The latter modifies the verbal action and gives it the colour of the noun by means of the qualificative: the adverb directs it and indicates its use. Thus, *gently, strongly, obediently* are modificatives; they indicate that the action is done in a manner, gentle, strong, obedient: *above, below, before, after,* are adverbs: they show the direction of the action relative to things, persons, time, place, number or measure.

When the modern grammarians have said, in speaking of adverbs such as those just cited, that they were *indeclinable,* I fear that following Latin forms, they may be mistaken in this as in many other things. I know well that the designative relation, for example, the article which inflects the noun, could not be inflected, unless there existed a new article for this use; I know well that the modificative could not be inflected either, since it contains an implied action which can only be developed by the verb; but I also know that an adverbial relation, a veritable relation becoming a noun by a simple deduction of thought, must be subject to inflection. I can go further. I say that a designative relation, an article, if it is made absolute, will experience a sort of inflection. Consider the adverbs *below, above, before, after, today, tomorrow,* etc., all these are capable of being inflected to a certain point. Does not one say: *bring that from below above;* place yourself *before;* speak only *after your opinion;* consider the usages *of today;* think *of tomorrow,* etc., etc.?

Nearly all the adverbial relations of the Hebraic tongue receive the articles and lend themselves to their movements. Many even have number and gender, as can be noticed among those here cited.

Adverbs of Place

אֵי : אַיֵּה :	where? where
אֵיפֹה : אֵיפוֹא :	where? wherein
פֹּא : פֹּה :	here, in this place
שָׁם :	there, in that place
מִפּוֹ : מִפֹּה : מִשָּׁם :	hence, whence
חוּץ :	outside
מִבַּיִת : בְּתוֹךְ :	inside, within
עֵבֶר : מֵעֵבֶר :	beyond
בֵּין : בֵּינַיִם :	between, among
עַל : מַעְלָה :	upon, on high
פְּנֵי : פָּנִים : לִפְנֵי :	in front of, facing
מַטָּה :	down, beneath
תַּחַת : מִתַּחַת :	below, from under
אַחַר : אַחֲרֵי :	after, behind
סָבִיב :	round about
הָלְאָה :	afar off *etc.*

Of Time

מָתַי : עַד־מָה :	when, how long
עַד :	until
אָז : אֲזַי :	then
עַתָּה :	now
עוֹד :	again
תָּמִיד :	continually
טֶרֶם :	before
יוֹמָם :	today
מָחָר : תְּמוֹל :	tomorrow, yesterday
מִלְּפָנִים	from before
מְהֵרָה :	quickly
	etc.

Of Number

אַף־כִּי :	how much more?	שֵׁשׁ :	six
אֶחָד :	one, first	שֶׁבַע :	seven
שְׁנֵי : שְׁנַיִם :	two, second	שְׁמֹנָה :	eight
שָׁלֹשׁ :	three	תֵּשַׁע :	nine
אַרְבַּע :	four	עֶשֶׂר :	ten
חָמֵשׁ :	five		*etc.*

Of Measure

אֵיךְ :	how?	מְאֹד :	very much
כֵּן : אָכֵן :	thus	שָׁוְא :	in vain
רַב :	enough	בְּלִי : מִבְּלִי :	nothing
מְעַט :	a little		*etc.*

ADVERBIAL RELATIONS

AFFIRMATIVE ADVERBS

אָמֵן : אָמְנָם   amen, verily   אַךְ :   wholly

כֹּה : כֵּן :   thus, so   etc.

SUSPENSIVE AND INTERROGATIVE

אוּלַי :   perhaps   אִם : הַאִם :   is it?

לָמָה :   why   פֶּן :   lest

לְמִן :   because   מַדּוּעַ :   therefore

לְמַעַן :   on account of   etc.

NEGATIVES

אַל :   not, no more   אַיִן : אֵינִי :   nothing

לֹא :   no, not   רֵיקָם :   empty

בַּל : בְּלֹא :   no, not   etc.

It is easy to see in glancing through these adverbial relations that their purpose is, as I have said, to show the employment of the action, its direction, its measure, its presence or its absence; and not to modify it. The action is modified by the modificative nouns. In the tongues where few nouns exist as in Hebrew for example, then the verbal form assists. This form which I have called intensive, lends itself to the intention of the writer, receives the movement of the sentence and gives to the verb the colour of the circumstance. This is what an intelligent translator ought never to lose sight of in the idioms of the Orient.

The reader who follows with close attention the progress of my grammatical ideas, should perceive that after having traversed the circle of the developments of speech, under the different modifications of the noun and the verb, we return to the sign from which we started: for the adverbial relation with which we are at the moment occupied, differs little from the designative relation and even mingles with it in many common expressions. I have already indicated this analogy, so that one can observe, when the time comes, the point where the circle of speech returning to itself, unites its elements.

This point merits attention. It exists between the affirmative and negative adverb; between *yes* and *no*, אך and אל or כה and לא: the substance and the verb: it can have nothing beyond. Whoever would reflect well upon the force of these two expressions, would see that they contain not alone the essence of speech but that of the universe, and that it is only by affirming or denying, wishing or not wishing, passing from nothingness to being or from being to nothingness, that the sign is modified, that speech is born, that intelligence is unfolded, that nature, that the universe moves toward its eternal goal.

I shall not dwell upon such speculations. I feel that to limit every tongue to two elementary expressions, would be too great a boldness in the state of our present grammatical knowledge. The mind encumbered with a multitude of words would hardly conceive a truth of this nature and would vainly attempt to bring back to elements so simple, a thing which appears to it so complicated.

But it can, however, be understood that the adverbial affirmation exists by itself in an absolute, independent manner, contained in the verb whose essence it constitutes: for every verb is affirmative: the negation is only its absence or its opposition. This is why, in any tongue whatsoever, to announce a verb is to affirm: to destroy it is to deny.

Sometimes without entirely destroying the verb one suspends the effect: then he interrogates. The Hebrew possesses two adverbial relations to illustrate this modification of speech: אם and הַאִם: it could be rendered by *is it?* but its usage is quite rare. The interrogation appears to have occurred most commonly in the tongue of Moses, as it still occurs among most of the meridional peoples: that is to say, by means of the accent of the voice.

ADVERBIAL RELATIONS

It indicates the meaning of the phrase. Sometimes, as I have said, the determinative article ה, takes an interrogative force.

The negation is expressed by means of the many adverbial relations that I have already given. Those most in use are לֹא and אֵין. The former expresses cessation, opposition, defense: the latter, absence and nothingness. These merit very particular attention.

Besides, all the adverbial relations without exception, are connected with the nominal and verbal affixes, and often form with them ellipses of great force. I am about to give some of these Hebraisms interpreting word-for-word when necessary.

אַיּוֹ ׃ אַיָּם ׃	where-of-him? where-of-them? (where is he, where are they?)
אַחֲרֶיךָ ׃	behind-thee
תַּחְתִּי ׃	under me (in my power)
בֵּינֵינוּ וּבֵינֶיךָ ׃ בֵּינָיִם ׃	between us and between thee: between them
לְפָנַי ׃ לְפָנֶיךָ ׃ לְפָנֵינוּ ׃	before me, before thee, before us
בַּעֲדִי ׃ בַּעֲדִיכֶם ׃ בַּעֲדֵיהֶם ׃	around me, around you, around them
עוֹדֵינוּ ׃ הַעוֹדָם ׃	again us (we are again) what! again them? (are they again?)
אִישׁ־הַבֵּנַיִם ׃	a man between (wavering between two parts).
אֶל־בִּינוֹת ׃ לַגַּלְגַּל ׃	toward the midst of the deep (toward the centre of ethereal spaces, of celestial spheres, of worlds)

מִבֵּינוֹת לַכְּרֻבִים: from between the cherubims (from the midst of that which represents the manifold forces)

INTERROGATION

מָה הוּא־לָהּ: what him-to her? (what did he say to her?)

מֶה חַטָּאתִי: what sin—mine? (what is my sin?)

אֶת־שׁוֹר מִי לָקַחְתִּי: of whom the ox I have taken? (whose is the ox that I have taken?)

בִּשְׁאוֹל מִי יוֹרֶה־לָּךְ: in Sheol who will point out to thee? (who will show thee?)

וּבֶן־אָדָם כִּי תִפְקְדֶנּוּ: and-the-son-of Adam thus shalt thou - visit - him? (shalt thou visit him thus, the son of Adam?)

מִי אָדוֹן לָנוּ: who is the Lord of us?

אֶשָּׂא עֵינַי אֶל־הֶהָרִים: shall I lift mine eyes unto these hills?

מֵאַיִן יָבוֹא עֶזְרִי: whence will come help to me?

אִם עֲוֹנוֹת תִּשְׁמָר־יָהּ: dost thou consider the iniquities, Jah!

NEGATION

אַל־תּוֹסֶף: thou shalt add no more

אַל־תָּצַר: thou shalt act no more vindictively

אַל־יֵרָא: he shall not see

ADVERBIAL RELATIONS

צִוִּיתִיךָ לְבִלִי אֲכָל׃	I commanded thee not to eat
בִּבְלִי אֲשֶׁר׃ עַל־בְּלִי׃	of nothing which... because not
לֹא מָצָא עֵזֶר׃	he found no help
לֹא־יִהְיֶה לְךָ אֱלֹהִים אֲחֵרִים׃	not shall-there-be-for-thee other Gods (there shall exist no other Gods for thee.)
לֹא תַעֲשֶׂה לְךָ פֶסֶל׃	thou shalt not make for thee any image
וְלֹא־יִהְיֶה עוֹד הַמַּיִם לְמַבּוּל׃	and-there shall not be again the waters of deluge. (the waters of deluge shall no more be raised)
לְבִלְתִּי הַכּוֹת אֹתוֹ׃	not to wound him
לֹא יָדַעְתִּי׃	I knew it not
וְאֵינֶנּוּ׃	and he is not
וְאֵינְךָ׃ וְאֵינֵימוֹ׃	and thou art not: and they are not
אֵין־יֵשׁ־רוּחַ בְּפִיהֶם׃	nothing being spirit in the-mouth-to-them (there was nothing spiritual in their mouth)
כִּי־אֵין הַמֶּלֶךְ יוּכַל אֶתְכֶם דָּבָר׃	for nothing of the king being able with you thing. (for there is nothing of the king which may be something with you)
וְאֵין רוֹאֶה וְאֵין יוֹדֵעַ וְאֵין מֵקִיץ׃	and nothing seeing, and nothing knowing and nothing watching (he saw and he knew and he watched nothing)

269

| כִּי אֵין בַּמָּוֶת זִכְרֶךָ: | for nothing in death to remember thee (there is no memory in death of thou who survives) |
| יְהֹוָה אַל־בְּאַפְּךָ תוֹכִיחֵנִי: | Yahweh no more in the wrath thine shalt thou chastise me (chastise me no more in thy wrath) |

PARAGOGIC CHARACTERS

§ III.

Paragogic Characters

The thinkers of the last centuries in their innumerable labours concerning the tongue of the Hebrews, many of which are not without merit, must have seen that the Hebraic characters had nearly all an intrinsic value, which gave force to the words to which they were added. Although the majority of these savants were very far from going back to the origin of the sign, and although nearly all of them discerned that the meaning attached to these characters was arbitrary, they could nevertheless, detect it. Some, considering more particularly those characters which appear at the beginning or the end of words to modify the signification, have chosen six: א, ה, י, מ, נ and ת: and taking the sound which results from their union, have designated them by the barbarous name of *hééманthes*. Others, selecting only those which chance appears to insert in certain words or to add them without evident reason, have named them *paragogics;* that is to say, *happened*. These characters, likewise six in number are: א, ה, י, ו, נ and ת. The only difference which exists between the *hééманthes* and the *paragogics*, is in the latter, where the vowel ו is substituted for the consonant מ.

I might omit further discussion of these characters since I have already considered them under the relation of signs; but in order to leave nothing to be desired, I shall state concisely what the Hebraists have thought of them.

א In considering this character as belonging to the *hééманthes*, the Hebraists have seen that it expressed force, stability, duration of substance, denomination. As *paragogic*, they have taught that it was found without motives, added to certain verbal tenses which terminate in ו, as in the following examples:

הָלְכוּא   they went   נָשׂוּא   they raised

בוּא   they wished   · etc.

This addition is a sort of redundancy in imitation of the Arabs. It expresses the force and duration of the action.

ה Whether this character is ranked among the *héémanthes*, or among the *paragogics* it is useless for me to add anything more to what I have said, either as sign, or as determinative or emphatic article. We know now that it can begin or terminate all kinds of words, nouns, verbs or relations.

ו It is not a question here of its astonishing power of changing the temporal modifications of the verbs, by carrying to the past those which are of the future, and to the future those which are of the past. When the Hebraists called it *paragogic*, they considered it simply as added to certain words without other reasons than of joining them together.

וְחַיְתוֹ־אֶרֶץ׃   the terrestrial animality (the animal kingdom)

בְּנוֹ־בְעוֹר׃   the son of Beor

לְמַעְיְנוֹ־מָיִם׃   the source of the waters

י The Hebraists who have considered this character as *héémanthe*, have attributed to it the same qualities as the vowel א, but more moral and bearing more upon mind than upon matter. Those who have treated it as *paragogic* have said that it was found sometimes inserted in words and oftener placed at the end, particularly in the feminine. They have not given the cause of this insertion or this addition, which results very certainly from the faculty that

PARAGOGIC CHARACTERS 273

it has as sign, of expressing the manifestation and the imminence of actions. For example:

לִדְרוֹשׁ׃ with a view to being informed, being instructed; to inquire

תִּיעָשֶׂה׃ מִיאָתִי׃ it will be done without interruption: by myself, openly

רַבָּתִיעָם׃ הַחֵצִי׃ an immense crowd of people: a swift arrow

מְקִימִי׃ establishing him with glory

אֹיְבָתִי׃ hostile with boldness

מ This character placed among the *héémanthes* by the Hebraists is found equally at the beginning and the end of words. When it is at the beginning it becomes, according to them, local and instrumental; it forms the names of actions, passions and objects. When it is at the end it expresses that which is collective, comprehensive, generic, or more intense and more assured. It is very singular that with these ideas, these savants have been able so often to misunderstand this sign whose usage is so frequent in the tongue of Moses. What has caused their error is the readiness with which they have confused it with the verbal affix מ. I shall produce in my notes upon the Cosmogony of Moses, several examples wherein this confusion has caused the strangest mistranslation. Here for instance, are some examples without comment.

אָמְנָם׃ a truth universal; a faith immutable

יוֹמָם׃ שְׁמָם׃ all the day; a name collective, generic, universal

אֹתָם׃ the whole; the collective self-sameness; the ipseity

עוֹלָם׃ the universality of time, space, duration, ages

נָחָם׃ he ceased entirely; he rested wholly

בְּשֻׁנָם׃ in the general action of declining, of being lost

מַשְׁחִיתָם׃ to degrade, to destroy, to ruin entirely

נ Among the *héémanthes*, this character expresses either passive action and turns back to itself when it appears at the beginning of words; or, unfoldment and augmentation when it is placed at the end. Among the *paragogics*, it is added without reason, say the Hebraists, to the verbal modifications terminated by the vowels ו or י; or is inserted in certain words to soften the pronunciation. It is evident that even in this case it retains its character as can be judged by the following examples.

יָדְעוּן׃ they knew at full length
תַּעֲשִׂין׃ thou shalt do without neglecting
לִתֵּן׃ so as to give generously
יְסֹבְבֶנְהוּ׃ he surrounded it well
יִצְּרֶנְהוּ׃ he closed it carefully
יֶשְׁנוֹ׃ behold his manner of being (his being)
יָגוֹן׃ torment of the soul, sorrow, entire disorganization
זִכְרוֹן׃ steadfast remembrance, very extended
בִּצָּרוֹן׃ well-stored provisions

ת The Hebraists who have included this character among the *héémanthes*, have attributed to it the property that it has as sign, of expressing the continuity of things and their reciprocity. Those who have made it a *paragogic* have only remarked the great propensity that it has for being substituted for the character ה; propensity of which I have spoken sufficiently. Here are some examples relative to its reciprocity as sign:

תּוּגָה׃ reciprocal sorrow
תְּנוּאָה׃ mutual estrangement, aversion
תָּאַב׃ he desired mutually and continually
תְּנוּמָה׃ sympathetic sleep
תַּגְמוּל׃ mutual retribution, contribution

§ IV.

Conclusion.

This is about all that the vulgar Hebraists have understood of the effects of the sign. Their knowledge would have been greater if they had known how to apply it. But I do not see one who has done so. It is true that in the difficulties which they found in the triliteral and dissyllabic roots, they applied, with a sort of devotion to the Hebraic tongue, this application which already very difficult in itself, obtained no results.

I venture to entertain the hope that the reader who has followed me with consistent attention, having reached this point in my Grammar, will no longer see in the tongues of men so many arbitrary institutions, and in speech, a fortuitous production due to the mechanism of the organs alone. Nothing arbitrary, nothing fortuitous moves with this regularity, or is developed with this constancy. It is very true that without organs man would not speak; but the principle of speech exists none the less independently, ever ready to be modified when the organs are suspectible of this modification. Both the principle and the organs are equally given, but the former, exists immutable, eternal, in the divine essence; the latter, more or less perfect according to the temporal state of the substance from which they are drawn, present to this principle, points of concentration more or less homogeneous and reflect it with more or less purity. Thus the light strikes the crystal which is to receive it and is refracted with an energy analogous to the polish of its surface. The purer the crystal the more brilliant it appears. A surface unpolished, sullied or blackened, gives only an uncertain dull reflection or none at all. The light remains immutable although its refracted rays may be infinitely varied. In this manner is the principle of speech developed. Ever the same *au fond*, it indicates nevertheless, in its effects the organic state of man. The more this state acquires perfection, and it acquires it unceasingly, the more speech gives facility to display its beauties.

According as the centuries advance, everything advances toward its perfection. Tongues experience in this respect, the vicissitudes of all things. Dependent upon the organs as to form, they are independent as to principle. Now this principle tends toward the unity from which it emanates. The multiplicity of idioms is a reflection upon the imperfection of the organs since it is opposed to this unity. If man were perfect, if his organs had acquired all the perfection of which they were susceptible, one single tongue would extend and be spoken from one extremity of the earth to the other.

I feel that this idea, quite true as it is, will appear paradoxical; but I cannot reject the truth.

From the several simple tongues I have chosen the Hebrew to follow its developments and make them perceived. I have endeavoured to reveal the material of this ancient idiom, and to show that my principal aim has been to make its genius understood and to induce the reader to apply this same genius to other studies; for the sign upon which I have raised my grammatical edifice is the unique basis upon which repose all the tongues of the world.

The sign comes directly from the eternal principle of speech, emanated from the Divinity, and if it is not presented everywhere under the same form and with the same attributes, it is because the organs, charged with producing it exteriorly, not only are not the same among all peoples, in all ages and under all climates, but also because they receive an impulse which the human mind modifies according to its temporal state.

The sign is limited to the simple inflections of the voice. There are as many signs possible as inflections. These inflections are few in number. The people who have distinguished them from their different combinations, representing them by characters susceptible of being linked together, as one sees it in the literal alphabet which we possess, have hastened the perfecting of the language with respect to the exterior forms; those who, blending them with these same combinations have applied them to an indefinite series of compound characters, as one sees among the Chinese, have perfected its interior images. The Egyptians who possessed at once the literal sign and the hieroglyphic combination, became, as they certainly were in the temporal state of things, the most enlightened people of the world.

The different combinations of signs constitute the roots. All roots are monosyllabic. Their number is limited; for it can never be raised beyond the combinations possible between two consonant signs and one vocal at the most. In their origin they presented only a vague and generic idea applied to all things of the same form, of the same species, of the same nature. It is always by a restriction of thought that they are particularized. Plato who considered general ideas as preëxistent, anterior to particular ideas, was right even in reference to the formation of the words which express them. Vegetation is conceived before the vegetable, the vegetable before the tree, the tree before the oak, the oak before all the particular kinds. One sees animality before the animal, the animal before the quadruped, the quadruped before the wolf, the wolf before the fox or the dog and their diverse races.

At the very moment when the sign produces the root, it produces also the relation.

Particular ideas which are distinguished from general ideas, are assembled about the primitive roots which thenceforth become idiomatic, receive the modifications of the sign, combine together and form that mass of words which the different idioms possess.

Nevertheless the unique verb until then implied, appropriates a form analogous to its essence and appears in speech. At this epoch a brilliant revolution takes place in speech. As soon as the mind of man feels it, he is penetrated by it. The substance is illumined. The verbal life circulates. Thousands of nouns which it animates become particular verbs.

Thus speech is divided into substance and verb. The substance is distinguished by gender and by number, by quality and by movement. The verb is subject to movement and form, tense and person. It expresses the different affections of the will. The sign, which transmits all its force to the relation, binds these two parts of speech, directs them in their movements and constructs them.

Afterward all depends upon the temporal state of things. At first a thousand idioms prevail in a thousand places on the earth. All have their local physiognomy. All have their particular genius. But nature obeying the unique impulse which it receives from the Being of beings, moves on to unity. Peoples, pushed toward one another like waves of the ocean, rush and mingle together, losing the identity of their natal idiom. A tongue more extended is formed. This tongue becomes enriched, is coloured and propagated. The sounds become softened by contact and use. The expressions are numerous, elegant, forceful. Thought is developed with facility. Genius finds a docile instrument. But one, two or three rival tongues are equally formed; the movement which leads to unity continues. Only, instead of some weak tribes clashing, there are entire nations whose waves now surge, spreading from the north to the south and from the Orient to the Occident. Tongues are broken like political existences. Their fusion takes place. Upon their common *débris* rise other nations and other tongues more and more extended, until at last one sole nation prevails whose tongue enriched by all the discoveries of the past ages, child and just inheritor of all the idioms of the world, is propagated more and more, and takes possession of the earth.

O France! O my Country! art thou destined to so great glory? Thy tongue, sacred to all men, has it received from heaven enough force to bring them back to unity of Speech? It is the secret of Providence.

PREFATORY NOTE

After all that I have said in my Grammar, both concerning the force of the sign and the manner in which it gives rise to the root, there remains but little to be added. The strongest argument that I can give in favour of the truths that I have announced upon this subject, is undoubtedly the Vocabulary which now follows. I venture to say that the attentive and wisely impartial reader will see with an astonishment mingled with pleasure, some four or five hundred primitive roots, all monosyllables resulting easily from the twenty-two signs, by twos, according to their vocal or consonantal nature, developing all universal and productive ideas and presenting a means of composition as simple as inexhaustible. For as I have already said, and as I shall often prove in my notes, there exists not a single word of more than one syllable, which is not a compound derived from a primitive root, either by the amalgamation of a mother vowel, the adjunction of one or several signs, the union of the roots themselves, the fusion of one in the other, or their contraction.

This great simplicity in the principles, this uniformity and this surety in the course, this prodigious richness of invention in the developments, had caused the ancient sages of Greece, those capable of understanding and appreciating the remains of the sacred dialect of Egypt, to think that this dialect had been the work of the priests themselves who had fashioned it for their own use; not perceiving, from the irregular turn pursued by the Greek idiom and even the vulgar idiom then in use in Lower Egypt, that any tongue whatsoever, given its own full sway, might attain to this degree of perfection. Their error was to a certain point excusable. They could not know, deprived as they were of means of comparison, the enormous difference which exists between a real mother tongue and one which is not. The merit of the Egyptian priests was not, as has been supposed, in having invented the ancient idiom, which they used instead of the sacred dialect, but in having fathomed the genius, in having well understood its elements, and in having been instructed to employ them in a manner conformable with their nature.

The reader will discern, in glancing through the Vocabulary which I give and which I have restored with the utmost care possible, to what degree of force, clarity and richness, the tongue whose basis it formed, could attain; he will also perceive its usefulness in the hands of the wise and studious man, eager to go back to the origin of speech and to sound the mystery, hitherto generally unknown, of the formation of language.

The universal principle is not for man. All that falls beneath his senses, all that of which he can acquire a real and positive understanding is diverse. God alone is one. The principle which presides at the formation of the Hebrew is not therefore universally the same as that which presides at the formation of Chinese, Sanskrit or any other similar tongue. Although issued from a common source which is Speech, the constitutive principles of the tongues differ. Because a primitive root formed of such or such sign, contains such a general idea in Hebrew, it is not said for that reason that it ought to contain it in Celtic. Very close attention must be given here. This same root can, on the contrary, develop an opposite idea; and this occurs nearly always when the spirit of a people is found in contradiction with that of another people concerning the sentiment which is the cause of the idea. If a person, reading my Vocabulary, seeing the most extended developments follow the simplest premises, and discovering at first glance irresistible relations in Hebrew with his own language and the ancient or modern tongues which he knows, ventures to believe that Hebrew is the primitive tongue from which all the others descend, he would be mistaken. He would imitate those numberless systematic scholars who, not understanding the vast plan upon which nature works have always wished to restrict it to the narrow sphere of their understanding.

It is not enough to have grasped the outline of one single figure to understand the arrangement of a picture. There is nothing so false, from whatever viewpoint one considers it, as that impassioned sentence which has become a philosophic axiom: *ab uno disce omnes*. It is in following this idea that man has built so many heterogeneous edifices upon sciences of every sort.

The Radical Vocabulary which I give is that of Hebrew; it is therefore good primarily for the Hebrew; secondarily, for the tongues which belong to the same stock, such as Arabic, Coptic, Syriac, etc; but it is only in the third place and in an indirect manner that it can be of use in establishing the etymologies of Greek or Latin, because these two tongues having received their first roots from the ancient Celtic, have with Hebrew only coincidental relations given them by the universal principle of speech, or the fortuitous mixture of peoples: for the Celtic, similar to Hebrew, Sanskrit and Chinese in all that comes from the universal principle of speech, differs essentially in the particular principle of its formation.

The French, sprung from the Celtic in its deepest roots, modified by a mass of dialects, fashioned by Latin and Greek, inundated by Gothic, mixed with Frank and Teutonic, refashioned by Latin, repolished by Greek, in continual struggle with all the neighbouring idioms; the French is perhaps, of all the tongues extant today upon the face of the earth, the one whose etymology is most difficult. One cannot act with too much circumspection in this matter. This tongue is beautiful but its beauty lies not in its simplicity: on the contrary, there is nothing so complicated. It is in proportion as one is enlightened concerning the elements which compose it, that the difficulty of its analysis will be felt and that unknown resources will be discovered. Much time and labour is necessary before a good etymological dictionary of this tongue can be produced. Three tongues well understood, Hebrew, Sanskrit and Chinese can, as I have said, lead one to the origin of speech; but to penetrate into the etymological details of

French, it would be necessary to know also the Celtic, and to understand thoroughly all the idioms which are derived therefrom and which directly or indirectly have furnished expressions to that of the Gauls, our ancestors, of the Romans, our masters, or of the Franks, their conquerors. I say to understand thoroughly, for grammars and vocabularies ranged in a library do not constitute real knowledge. I cannot prove better this assertion than by citing the example of Court de Gébelin. This studious man understood Greek and Latin well, he possessed a slight knowledge of the oriental tongues as much as was possible in his time; but as he was ignorant of the tongues of the north of Europe or at least as their genius was unfamiliar to him, this defect always prevented his grasping in their real light, French etymologies. The first step which he took in this course, was an absurd error which might have brought entire discredit upon him if there had been anyone capable of detecting his mistake. He said, for example, that the French word *abandon* was a kind of elliptical and figurative phrase composed of three words *a-ban-don;* and that it signified a gift made to the people, taking the word *ban* for the people, the public. Besides it is not true that the word *ban* may signify *people* or *public* in the sense in which he takes it, since its etymology proves that it has signified *common* or *general*,[1] it was not necessary to imagine an ellipsis of that force to explain *abandon*. It is only necessary to know that in Teutonic *band* is a

---

[1] We still say *banal* to express that which is *common*. It is worthy of notice that the word *banal* goes back to the Gallic root *ban*, which in a restricted sense characterizes *a woman;* whereas its analogues *common* and *general* are attached, the one to the Celtic root *gwym*, *cwym* or *kum*, and the other to the Greek root Γυν, which is derived from it; now these two roots characterize alike, *a woman*, and all that which is *joined*, *united*, *communicated*, or *generated*, *produced*. *Cym* in Gallic-Celtic, Συν or Συμ in Greek, *cum* in Latin, serves equally the designative or adverbial relation, to express *with*. The Greek word γαμεῖν signifies to be *united*, to *marry*, to *take wife*, and the word *gemein* which, in modern German holds to the same root, is applied to all that is *common, general*.

root expressing all that is *linked, retained, guarded,* and that the word *ohn* or *ohne,* analogous to the Hebrew אִין is a negation which being added to words, expresses absence. So that the compound *band-ohne* or *aband-ohn,* with the redundant vowel, is the exact synonym of our expressions *abandon* or *abandoment.*

Court de Gébelin made a graver mistake when he wrote that the French word *vérité* is derived from a so-called primitive root *var,* or *ver,* which according to him signified *water* and all that which is limpid and transparent as that element: for how could he forget that in the Celtic and in all the dialects of the north of Europe the root *war, wer, wir,* or *wahr, ward,* develops the ideas of being, in general, and of man in particular, and signifies, according to the dialect, that which *is,* that which *was,* and even becomes a sort of auxiliary verb to express that which *will be?* It is hardly conceivable.

Now if a savant so worthy of commendation has been able to go astray upon this point in treating of French etymologies, I leave to the imagination what those who lack his acquired knowledge would do in this pursuit.

Doubtless there is nothing so useful as etymological science, nothing which opens to the meditation a field so vast, which lends to the history of peoples so sure a link; but also, nothing is so difficult and nothing which demands such long and varied preparatory studies. In the past century when a writer joined to Latin, certain words of Greek and of bad Hebrew, he believed himself a capable etymologist. Court de Gébelin was the first to foresee the immensity of the undertaking. If he has not traversed the route he has at least had the glory of showing the way. Notwithstanding his mistakes and his inadvertencies which I have disclosed with an impartial freedom, **he is still the only guide that one can follow, so far as general maxims are concerned, and the laws to be observed in the exploration of tongues.** I cannot conceive how a writer who appears to unite so much positive learning as the one who has just published a book in German full of excellent views upon the tongue and science of the Indians[1] can have misunderstood the first rules of etymology to the point of giving constantly for roots of Sanskrit, words of two, three and four syllables; not knowing or feigning not to know that every root is monosyllabic; still less can I conceive how he has not seen that, in the comparison of tongues, it is never the compound which proves an original analogy, but the root. Sanskrit has without doubt deep connection with ancient Celtic and consequently with Teutonic, one of its dialects; but it is not by analyzing about thirty compound words of modern German that these connections are proved. To do this one must go back to the primitive roots of the two tongues, show their affinity, and in compounds, inevitably diverse, distinguish their different genius and give thus to the philosopher and historian, materials for penetrating the *esprit* of these two peoples and noting their moral and physical revolutions.

In this Prefatory Note, my only object has been to show the difficulty of the etymological science and to warn the overzealous reader as much as possible, against the wrong applications that he might make in generalizing particular principles, and against the errors into which too much impetuosity might lead him.

[1] *Ueber die Sprache und Weisheit der Indier*... I vol. in-8 Heidelberg. 1808.

This is the end of this publication.

Any remaining blank pages are for our book binding requirements and are blank on purpose.

To search thousands of interesting publications like this one, please remember to visit our website at:

http://www.kessinger.net

CPSIA information can be obtained
at www.ICGtesting.com
Printed in the USA
LVHW052201230223
740261LV00036B/448